Better
Homes
and Gardens®

Landscaping
Gardening Made Easy

Meredith® Consumer Marketing
Des Moines, Iowa

Better Homes and Gardens.

Landscaping
Gardening Made Easy

MEREDITH CONSUMER MARKETING
Vice President, Consumer Marketing: Janet Donnelly
Consumer Marketing Product Director: Heather Sorensen
Consumer Marketing Product Manager: Wendy Merical
Business Director: Ron Clingman
Senior Production Manager: Al Rodruck

WATERBURY PUBLICATIONS, INC.
Contributing Editor: Karen Weir-Jimerson, Studio G, Inc.
Contributing Copy Editor: Carrie Schmitz
Contributing Proofreader: Peg Smith
Contributing Indexer: Donald Glassman

Editorial Director: Lisa Kingsley
Creative Director: Ken Carlson
Associate Editors: Tricia Bergman, Mary Williams
Associate Design Director: Doug Samuelson
Production Assistant: Mindy Samuelson

BETTER HOMES AND GARDENS® MAGAZINE
Editor in Chief: Gayle Goodson Butler
Managing Editor: Gregory H. Kayko
Creative Director: Michael D. Belknap
Deputy Editor, Gardening: Eric Liskey

MEREDITH NATIONAL MEDIA GROUP
President: Tom Harty

MEREDITH CORPORATION
Chairman and Chief Executive Officer: Stephen M. Lacy

In Memoriam: E.T. Meredith III (1933–2003)

Pictured on the front cover:
top left An inviting curved brick walkway adds curb appeal.
bottom left Stone walls are natural ways to solve sloped areas your yard.
right Shaded gardens can come alive with color when you plant colorful perennials such as astilbe and hosta.

Copyright © 2014
Meredith Corporation.
Des Moines, Iowa.
First Edition.
Printed in the United States of America.
ISBN: 978-0-696-30185-8

All of us at Meredith® Consumer Marketing are dedicated to providing you with information and ideas to enhance your home. We welcome your comments and suggestions. Write to us at: Meredith Consumer Marketing, 1716 Locust St., Des Moines, IA 50309-3023.

Contents

Chapter 1

Chapter 2

Chapter 3

84
CREATIVE LANDSCAPE PLANTINGS

Trees, shrubs, perennials, and roses make a diverse landscape.

Chapter 4

124
MAINTAINING YOUR LANDSCAPE

Keep your landscape looking great.

Chapter 5

146
DREAM LANDSCAPES GALLERY

Get inspiration for your own landscape projects.

CHAPTER ONE

Landscape Design

Make your yard a beautiful haven that best fits your region and enhances your lifestyle.

Garden Design

Creating the landscape of your dreams starts with versing yourself in some essential elements of design.

Like a trowel and a spade required for gardening, the basic elements of garden design provide you with tools for making the best garden possible. These artistic principles take the mystery out of garden design. Choose and combine your plants and other landscape features on the basis of these elements—just as a professional designer would—for the most beautiful scheme.

Even if you work with a professional to develop your garden design, understanding these principles helps you speak the pro's language and benefits the final results.

Line

One of the most important design elements, line involves everything in the garden. Think about the trunk of a tree, the distant horizon, or the transition from lawn to where the adjacent woods begin. Sidewalks, driveways, and fences are all lines in the landscape. As you plan and design your garden, always consider the line that is created by whatever you add.

There are four main ways to describe lines: curved, straight, horizontal, and vertical. None is more important than the others—each has different effects.

Curved lines shape informal garden beds and add interest to pathways. Straight lines evoke a sense of order and a crispness that is more formal. Soothing horizontal lines offer a sense of stability. Think of the ocean and how its wide expanse meets the sky, creating irrefutable peacefulness and majesty. Vertical lines project strength and movement.

No matter what types of lines you use, be aware that they lead the eye. Lines going away from you on the ground draw you

forward. Horizontal lines on the ground slow you down. Vertical lines lead the eye up and out of the garden. Curving lines take the eye on a journey. All line types are desirable and useful in a landscape when used in the right way. It's up to you to create where the lines will lead the eye and what you will see when you follow them.

Light

What could be more lovely than early morning or evening in the garden, when plants virtually glow from warm backlighting?

Light and shade change the way colors look and how they work together. Although you can't control natural light, you can play up its effects. Bright light has the same impact as warm color—it advances visually, making an object or area feel closer than it really is.

Light can be either natural or artificial. It is easy to add a low-voltage lighting system to extend your garden enjoyment into the evening hours. Various fixtures and their positioning create different effects. Frontlighting a dark area highlights a particular feature. Backlighting silhouettes a sculpture, tree, or shrub. Sidelighting, which can also produce dramatic effects, is used mostly for safety along walks and paths.

Texture

Texture evokes emotional responses. Both tactile and visual textures create an impulse to reach out and touch. Use texture to contrast plants in groups or minimize architectural lines.

The characteristics of texture divide plants into three basic groups: coarse, medium, and fine. Coarse-texture plants, hardscaping materials, and garden structures have large or boldly tactile components, such as the leaves of rhubarb or an arbor made with rough-cut posts. Fine-texture materials include many ferns and grasses, or a delicate structure such as a bent-wire trellis or arbor. Medium textures fall in between.

Changes in texture can be subtle; the textures of various plants (and objects) are relative to one another. An ornamental grass, when viewed alone, may seem to have a fine texture.

opposite left Lines leading away from you tend to pull you along. The strong curve of this walk leads the eye along the path and to the front door. ***opposite above*** Before choosing a plant, shrub, or tree, picture its mature size, shape, and overall presence. Seasonal color, such as trees with fall color, is also a consideration. ***opposite middle*** Combine a range of fine-, medium-, and coarse-textured plants to achieve balance and a bit of drama. ***opposite below*** Tall structural objects such as arbors and trellises add height to the landscape.

Basics: Garden Design

However, when compared with zoysiagrass, which is much more finely textured, it may appear more coarse in texture.

You'll find lots of textures—smooth, prickly, ripply, frilly—and endless ways to combine them to achieve repetition, contrast, balance, and unity. All are found in a successful garden.

Often the textural appeal of plants is found in their leaves. Dainty-leaved plants make a staccato of dots; grasses, irises, and daylilies paint pleasant, smooth stripes. Smooth hostas paired with astilbe's feathery flowers and serrated foliage make a classic combination.

Form

A landscape without strong contrasting forms becomes as confusing as a melody without rhythm. The form and shape of plants and other objects in the garden work to divide space, enclose areas, and provide architectural interest. Grouping plants displays their shapes and creates various effects.

Round forms, such as boxwood or barberry shrubs, for instance, add definition and stability to a mixed border. A series of mounded forms creates an undulating rhythm.

Repeated narrow verticals also add stability. Alone, an upright arborvitae or a thin cactus looks awkward. Clustered, they appear well-placed. The strong uprights of a fence add a sense of security and completeness.

Scale

Scale, or proportion, is the size relationship of one object to another. A 30-foot tree is out of place in the middle of a small patio, but a dwarf tree makes sense. Conversely, a massive house overpowers a narrow front walk lined with strips of flowers.

Pattern

Pattern is the repetition of shapes in order. Pattern creates rhythm as well as charm. It reinforces texture and contrast.

When creating patterns, think of light and shadow as part of the palette. Use pattern to draw attention to an area; be careful not to overdo bold patterns, which can overwhelm. Also apply this principle when creating backgrounds. Lay bricks in a herringbone pattern in walkways, patios, entryways, and driveway borders to unify your hardscape, for example. Employ pattern to direct people through the garden too.

Balance

Visual balance is achieved when the elements on each side of a real or imaginary axis are equal. If too much emphasis is placed on one side of the garden, your eye will be drawn more readily there and not to the garden as a whole.

There are two basic types of balance: symmetrical (formal) and asymmetrical (informal). When establishing balance, you need to determine a central reference point from which to draw an axis. It could be the front door, a tree in the backyard, or another object.

Symmetrical, or formal, balance is the easiest to see and understand: The elements on either side of a real or imaginary line are mirror images.

Formal balance doesn't always suit a home or garden style. You may prefer informal, or asymmetrical, balance. For example, a large tree on the left can be balanced by three smaller ones on the right. Or a large mass of cool colors on one side can balance a small mass of hot colors on the other side.

Unity

Unity results when all of the basic garden design principles come together in a balanced, harmonious whole. Focusing on harmony will help as you choose from an exciting and sometimes bewildering array of plants and other landscaping materials.

Make simplicity a guidepost as well, and you likely will achieve a unified design that gives you a sense of completeness. Good structure in the overall design, combined with hardscape that meets your needs for service and enjoyment, creates the perfect setting into which you can place favorite plants—trees, shrubs, groundcovers, flowers, and seasonal containers.

opposite above Symmetrical, or formal, balance is accomplished when one side of a setting is balanced by a mirror image on the opposite side. *opposite left* Whether the landscape is large or small, it is important to have perspective on the scale of the elements. Note that in this well-conceived setting, the circular pads get smaller as you approach the small statue. *opposite middle* Informal, or asymmetrical, balance is achieved by using different but equally weighted objects in a design. *opposite right* Repeating colors in a landscape create a sense of unity.

11

Basics: Garden Design

Contrast

Contrast emphasizes the difference between a plant or an object and its surroundings. Using contrast is the best way to avoid predictability in a garden. It also adds a pleasing sense of tension between elements. Like most garden design principles, contrast is good in moderation; too much can be confusing and unrelaxing to the eye.

You can create contrast by manipulating various elements, such as form, texture, and color. Achieve a distinctive look by planting the contrasting forms of horizontal 'Bar Harbor' juniper in front of red-twig dogwood, for instance.

You can contrast textures by varying hardscaping materials, such as bricks and gravel, or plant textures, such as a leathery-leaved magnolia, next to a finely needled cedar or juniper shrub.

Color

Color seduces the eye, evokes mood, and reflects the seasons. As a powerful and unifying tool, color has predictable effects. Cool blues, purples, and greens soothe and recede, whereas warm reds, oranges, and yellows enliven and advance.

Single-color schemes enchant with their simplicity. The real fun comes in expressing your personality by combining colors. Some colors compete for attention; others harmonize.

Although flowers are the jewels of the garden, too many colors look chaotic. A balance of subtly different colors creates a pleasing effect.

Rhythm

Rhythm and repetition come about when you correctly position or contrast features. Rhythm prevents monotony.

Gardens that are complete in almost every sense may seem ordinary until rhythm is introduced. For instance, a stately procession of shade trees along a drive or the repetition of pavers or the pickets in a fence create a clear sense of movement.

above left The contrast of a teal-blue door draws attention. The door's dramatic color is accentuated further by the contrasting pink flowers. **left** Color contrast adds variety and interest. Colors opposite each other on the color wheel, such as purple and yellow, create strong contrast.

Rhythm doesn't require literal repetition. It may be achieved by the use of line. The path shown *center right* undulates with similar—although not exact—curves. In addition, the consistent use of the vertical lines of trees, shrubs, and standing stones *below right* helps create a sense of rhythm.

Another example of rhythm is the gradual change along a planting bed of warm colors and coarse textures to cool colors and fine textures, then back to warm and coarse. As different plants come into bloom and recede, to be replaced by others, there continues a satisfying sense of visual rhythm.

Variety

Just as you choose your guests for a dinner party with concern for their interests and personalities, you can combine a variety of plants for compatibility.

Similar shapes and colors reinforce a theme. But certain focal points, by virtue of their interesting character, deserve major attention. These focal points should stand out from the rest of the garden. Occasional accents, such as an arbor, a sculpture, or a specimen plant, create balance in a garden between the reference points and the background.

The elements of great design involve interaction. Color, form, and texture can combine to create a captivating scene.

top right Repeating a form helps to unify a garden. Even if these arbors were placed throughout the garden rather than in a line, a sense of unity would result. **above right** The rhythm of repeated shapes—such as the curves of the undulating path—leads the eye and suggests movement. **right** Accents add interesting variety to the garden; use them sparingly to maximize their individual impact.

Basics
Design Inspiration

Draw up a plan that capitalizes on the good elements of your site—one that helps disguise or solve problems.

The best inspiration for a beautiful landscape with gorgeous gardens is a purpose that drives and motivates decisions, actions, and choices. When your focus is firmly resolved, the rest of the garden falls naturally into place.

Identify your goal
Why do you want to change your landscape? The reasons might revolve around wanting to improve a view or add curb appeal to your yard. Or you might want a specialty garden because you have a passion for fresh flowers or a desire to attract birds and butterflies.

Your rationale might involve problem-solving, such as hiding an eyesore, or you might want to swap a water-guzzling lawn for drought-tolerant perennials. Perhaps you have a side yard that's overlooked and neglected. Or you no longer need a play area.

Consider multiple priorities for your landscape—a primary focus, and then secondary reasons you want to change and enhance your landscape.

Determine your style
Formal or casual, old-fashioned or modern, alpine or cottage—there might be as many garden styles as there are gardeners. Choose a style that complements your home—or not. If you're converting an entire yard into gardens complete with structures, you can veer away from following a style that suits the location.

With front yard gardens, it's important to marry design to architecture. Select a cottage or prairie garden style for Craftsman-style bungalows or ranch homes. Xeriscape gardens complement Southwestern stucco and adobe homes; formal plantings with strong lines pair nicely with traditional colonial architecture.

Assess your landscape design
You can approach design by mastering the elements—line, form, texture, color—or by manipulating the principles. If you execute the principles well, the elements usually fall into place.

As you consider balance, think of trees, shrubs, plants, and objects in the landscape as having visual weight. Some items are tall and square; others are billowing and round. When you have balance in a garden setting, you have equilibrium among all the parts. The garden exudes a feeling of harmony and stability.

Imagine a central axis running through the center of the planting bed. Distribute the visual weight of objects in the planting bed equally on opposite sides of that axis, and you achieve balance.

If you concentrate on achieving balance, the look will be formal and possibly contrived. Aim to create a garden that's pleasing to your eye. Before you plant, consider the final look, either on paper or using potted perennials in the garden to see whether you have struck a point of balance. Most likely you will have, because our brains are wired to respond to balance.

Another aspect of balance is symmetry. In a symmetrical design, both sides of the planting bed are roughly equal in terms of the objects' visual weight. A pair of matching containers flanking a clematis-covered arbor embodies symmetry, as does a clump of coreopsis placed on either side of a delphinium. Symmetry is key to executing formal garden design.

opposite above A frontyard garden trades turf—and the maintenance chores that go with it—for year-round beauty. This garden includes torch lily and garden phlox, plants that beckon butterflies.

INVENTORY YOUR SITE

Before breaking ground, take an inventory of what your site offers so your garden can capitalize on and blend into existing features.

1 MAKE A SKETCH
Pencil a rough drawing of the area where you plan to put the garden. Be as accurate as possible, but don't worry about crafting a to-scale sketch. Mark permanent features, such as fences, paths, existing plants, and play areas.

2 SNAP PHOTOS
Take pictures from surrounding spots—including interior rooms—that provide viewing points for the garden. Include photos of areas bordering the garden site and anything that's especially attractive or problematic. Refer to these photos as you design the garden.

3 CREATE A MUST-HAVE LIST
This list should include your garden essentials: certain plants (especially trees or shrubs), large rocks, oversize containers, or fountains. Use this list to incorporate items that are on hand or in your budget.

4 MAKE A WISH LIST
This list should include elements you hope to introduce into your garden one day.

5 COMPLETE A SITE ANALYSIS
Record light exposure and other environmental conditions for your proposed site. This information will guide you as you choose plants.

Basics: Design Inspiration

Once you have defined the "why" behind your landscape design and have an idea about the style you want to pursue, it's time to begin sketching. Use a piece of plain or graph paper to draw an outline of your garden area. You don't need a plan that's drawn to scale, although a certain amount of accuracy makes planning easier. A scale that adapts well to perennials is 1 inch on paper is equal to 2 feet in the garden.

Inside and around the outline of your yard, sketch any trees, fences, or structures that interact with or affect the garden. Pencil in the line of the house in relationship to the garden. If you're designing the garden with reference to a deck, patio, or particular interior room, include that area on your drawing.

As you sketch a garden bed, divide it into thirds to make plant placement easy. With beds viewed from one side, stairstep perennials, filling the front third of the bed with low-growing plants, the middle third with mid-range plants, and the back third with taller plants. If you design an island bed that will be viewed from all sides, place the tallest plants in the center of the garden and step down height as you work toward the edges.

Note any particular aspects of the site on the drawing—wet spots, windy corners, proximity to trees, or sun exposure. Keep the worksheet handy as you begin to choose plants. You might even draft a short list of plant requirements, such as drainage and light, or characteristics, such as long bloom, to facilitate plant selection.

Select plants

Make a master list of plantings. Start with those you have on hand or can obtain from friends or neighbors, and include plants you intend to purchase. Avoid the mistake of trying to incorporate too many plant species. Repetition and larger clumps stage an eye-pleasing scene.

When creating a garden bed, arrange plants in order of height. As you fill in times of flowering and foliage interest, you'll notice gaps. Look for perennials and shrubs that flower and introduce foliage interest to the garden in all seasons. Remember not to plan heavy-flowering windows during seasons when you're typically out of town.

When you're ready, begin adding plants to your garden plan. Start with shrubs and perennials that offer the same color, either through flowers or foliage. Once you pencil in those plants, place companion perennials you want near them, slowly building combinations until the garden plan is complete.

PENNY-PINCHING DESIGN

Grow a perennial garden on a shoestring budget without skimping on results. Try a few—or all—of these tips to trim the investment in your first-year garden.

Find free plants. Get perennial divisions from friends or neighbors. Even strangers are often willing to share plants with new gardeners. Just ask.

Shop plant sales. Look for locally sponsored plant sales by civic groups, garden clubs, or church fellowships. Avoid sales with professionally grown plants; those perennials typically cost more.

Start small. Use a combination of seeds and small plants to jump-start the garden. Sow seeds of one type of perennial in a swath; tuck a few small plants of the same variety into that swath. The small plants will give first-year flowers; seed-grown plants will catch up in size and flower power the next year.

Plan for bloom. Pint-size or bare-root perennials flower the first year. Plan on a few of these in your garden. Include a couple larger plants of the same type for a showy splash right away.

opposite A striking monochromatic blend, such as these delphiniums and solitary clematis, often begins with one plant that catches the gardener's eye.

left A successful design starts with a theme of your choosing and a plan drawn on paper. Analyze your site, and then create bed outlines. **top** A pathway that curves out of sight is an intriguing way to lead visitors through the garden, encouraging exploration. **above** Consider the view of your garden from indoors. A well-placed focal point in the foreground can lead your eye to the beds beyond.

Basics: Design Inspiration

A sweeping perennial border and a confined perennial cottage bed have something in common: Both require decisions regarding garden shape and size. Sometimes, as with the confined cottage bed, you might not have much choice in the matter. Surrounding objects, such as structures, driveways, patios, or fences, might dictate dimensions.

In an open space, freedom to design a large border or island bed can overwhelm you as you wrestle with balancing garden dreams with budget or time constraints. To narrow your options, consider various possibilities for the bed. For instance, do you favor a formal or informal look? With a formal garden, you'll incorporate more straight lines than curves; with an informal style, you'll have more curves than straight edges.

Consider possible shapes. A simple shape, such as an oval, kidney bean, or half-circle, lets plantings shine.

Nearby objects might influence bed shape. A fence enclosing your yard is a natural backdrop for a perennial border that curves in and out along the straight edge. Or you might want to create your perennial bed against a structure, such as a garden shed or garage. A solid backdrop for a perennial border reduces airflow, which can increase chances of powdery mildew, a problem that plagues pincushion flower, garden phlox, and bee balm. In that planting situation, choose mildew-resistant varieties.

Form can follow function. For a perennial bed serving as a patio backdrop, you definitely want the bed to wrap around the patio. If you want a cutting garden, provide space for large clumps or even rows of perennials, leaving access to all points of the bed for easy flower-gathering. A garden intended to host wildlife should offer ample elbowroom for layers of plants to provide adequate shelter and food to critters—and nearby seating areas to offer handy vantage points for wildlife-watching.

Check interior views of proposed exterior beds. If you sit near a particular window in your home, arrange a perennial garden to enhance that view. By allowing inside and outside spaces to interact, the perennial garden becomes an integral part of your home's living experience.

Practical pointers

In most settings, property dimensions and structures will guide garden bed length. Bed width can vary, even within the same border. In beds less than 24 inches wide, planting layers are one or two plants deep. This limits plant-combination potential. A bed width of 36 inches permits consistently beautiful perennial layering.

HOW MANY PLANTS?

To determine how many plants you need for your garden, you must understand plant spacing. For example, when you place perennials in the garden bed, space them according to their mature size. If a plant spreads 24 inches, you should place it 24 inches from the plant beside it. If that same plant nestles against a fence or object (such as a birdbath), place it 12 inches away.

When you arrange young plants in a new garden, you'll see plenty of soil (or mulch) between plants. Don't react to that by planting perennials too tightly—you'll only wind up dividing and moving plants as they reach their mature size. Instead, fill in the gaps with annuals until perennials spread.

FRONT-YARD GARDEN TIPS

BHG TEST GARDEN TIP

Make a lasting first impression with a front yard garden. Follow these tips to welcome guests and greet passersby with perennial charm.

Establish order. Foster order by limiting the number of species (5–10), planting them in groups, and repeating them throughout the garden.

Think big. Plan for planting beds large enough to accommodate the mix of plants necessary to convey order.

Make it flow. Repeat plant forms and textures to unify the plantings.

Frame the door. Make the front door your focal point, and steer design lines in that direction.

Coordinate color. Select perennial foliage and flowers to complement your home's exterior or front-porch furnishings.

Region
Design for Where You Live

Consider a landscape plan that incorporates plants and materials from your region to maximize success and minimize cost.

A row of marigolds and a square of grassy lawn may be an easy way to landscape, but it's the kind of garden you can find in millions of backyards from Alaska to Florida. Besides, that sort of cookie-cutter landscape is just plain boring. For something a little more personal, even unusual, look around at Mother Nature for inspiration.

Choose native plantings

Your first step is selecting native plants. For ideas, check out regional gardening books and local conservation and wildlife society brochures. Also talk with your county extension service and knowledgeable garden center staffs. Check plant labels to see if ones you like are regional natives. For example, plants from the humid South can tolerate tough summer heat and humidity. Plants that are native to the North are able to withstand cold temperatures, along with ice and wind. When you use native plants in your landscape, you know these plants are acclimated to your region and will be more successful in the long run.

If a low-maintenance landscape is appealing to you, native plants are less likely to need extra care. In dry areas, natives are less thirsty. In wet areas, natives can thrive. Planting natives means you'll spend less time caring for your landscape plantings and more time enjoying them.

Consider historical roots

History plays a role too. New England and Southern gardens might still embrace brick-lined, formal garden designs popularized by English colonials. In the Southwest, gardens with adobe walls and drought-tolerant native plants look as though they've always been there. Midwestern gardens might take cues from their agricultural surroundings, using such decorative elements from the familiar landscape as a cupola from a barn as a flowerbed centerpiece. And landscapes in seaside locations or those near large lakes might incorporate nautical design elements.

Choose regional materials

Even basic building materials can have a regional tone. Pine needles, for example, are the perfect Southern or North Woods mulch. Crushed oyster shells make excellent paving material (and are plentiful) in seaside locations. Other materials such as local stone, found or quarried within miles of your home, are likely to blend in better with the natural landscape than those shipped from hundreds of miles away.

The best ideas for landscape design can be found by looking just beyond your backyard. Natural features—oceans, prairies, woodlands, deserts, and mountains—provide clues about plants that will thrive and how you can create a garden sympathetic to your region.

opposite A garden border planted alongside coastal waterways has to contend with gusts of wind and salty sea spray. Choose plants that can tolerate and excel in these tough conditions. **above** Matching plants to your environment, such as the native prairie coneflower, improves the odds of creating a successful and long-lasting landscape.

Region: Design for Where You Live

Seasides

Seaside gardens often boast stunning backdrops, but problematic conditions such as wind, salt, and sandy soil also prevail. With a careful selection of plants suited to withstand these conditions, a seaside garden can greatly enhance the beauty of any beach house.

Observe carefully how nature distributes the plants along a coastline. Low-growing, spreading flowers and grasses, for example, grow closest to the water; taller perennials and shrubs are farther away.

When planting a seaside garden, you will not only be creating a place of beauty, you'll be helping the environment. Seaside plants help stabilize the soil and prevent erosion. Seaweed, washed and chopped, makes a great soil amendment. Use materials from the ocean, such as shell marl (mixed with cement) to make walkways; use large shells and driftwood as artistic accents.

left A sun-loving cottage garden on the shore of a lake offer flowers for cutting all summer long. **above** A tall, informal hedge of trees along the waterline prevents erosion and shields cleome and tall phlox from wind. **opposite** Beds near the beach might need to be filled with high-quality soil rather than the local sand.

Region: Design for Where You Live

Prairies

Although most natural prairie areas are long gone—even in the prairie states—prairie and wildflower gardening has become enormously popular. Prairie gardens are casual and exuberant. Although they may look carefree, they do require planting and maintenance such as weeding. Most prairie plants, however, are fairly drought tolerant.

True prairies are composed of a mixture of native grasses and wildflowers, a formula that can be duplicated in your own prairie garden. There are many wildflower mixtures on the market that contain colorful European wildflowers, but these flowers can become invasive and pose a threat to the naturally occurring plant communities. For this reason, only native wildflowers— those that were found in true prairies—should be planted in these gardens.

You can also create beds and borders with hand-selected perennial flower species that are prairie standouts, such as purple coneflower and black-eyed Susan. Although prairies are a mix of plants, you can plant colorful prairie perennials in mass to enjoy large blocks of color in your landscape.

True prairie perennials, and those that are hybridized from these species, are hardy and beautiful. Flowering prairie natives include purple coneflower, black-eyed Susan, heleopsis, penstemon, monarda, goldenrod, and helenium. Grasses are also an essential element in a prairie garden and include little bluestem, big bluestem, Indian grass, and quaking grass.

Prairie gardens don't just love sunshine, they require it. There are no shade-loving prairie natives. To thrive and bloom, these plants must have at least six to eight hours of full sun every day. Afterall, historical prairies flourished in wide-open, sunny spaces.

Although prairie gardens often look wild and untamed, fences, walls, or even cut-grass pathways will help your mini prairie look well-tended. This rustic-style garden will provide you with hundreds of beautiful flowers for your garden and bouquets.

opposite above Many varieties, including purple coneflower, black-eyed Susan, and obedient plant, are ideal for sunny meadow plantings. **opposite left** A rustic fence reminiscent of split-rail fencing stirs memories of the pioneers who made their homes on the prairies a century or more ago. **opposite right** Although a picket fence and vintage metal gate aren't unique to America's prairies, they add a fitting down-home feel. **right** Accents carry out a regional theme. Here a small windmill and collection of well-loved watering cans look like they're straight off the farm.

Region: Design for Where You Live

Woodlands

Many areas of this country are (or were, before development took its toll) naturally occurring woodlands. But there is much more to a forest than trees. Observe carefully and you'll see a vertical garden with plants growing from 2 inches to 200 feet tall. Echo this in your own landscape by including trees, shrubs, and low-growing plants.

If you are starting a woodland garden from scratch, plant the trees first and install specimens as large as you can afford to get the effect you want as quickly as possible. Then fill in with understory shrubs, perennials, and annuals.

Most woodland flowers bloom in spring before the leaves of the trees above emerge and block the sun, but you can include many shade-loving nonnatives to stretch your blooming season. You can also include spring-flowering bulb species in woodland gardens that provide a natural and beautiful landscape in spring. Many narcissus varieties will naturalize, or spread, and carpet your woodland floor in blooms. Many woodland wildflowers are also spreaders. Woodland wildflowers include Dutchman's breeches, wild ginger, hepatica, Jack-in-the-pulpit, and dogtooth violet.

Creating a path—using wood chips, pine bark, pine straw, or other locally available organic mulch—will give your woodland garden design and direction (as well as a way to traverse the landscape). A winding path through a woodland garden can be an excellent way to interact with your garden by taking a walk through it every day.

Water features (natural or constructed) are another way to add dimension to a woodland garden. A small water garden or stream garden, both with circulating pump systems to keep the water clear, add the gentle sound of moving water. Water also attracts many wildlife species, from toads to birds.

Adding structures and seating to a woodland garden is easy. A rustic wooden bench or a rough-hewn pergola complement a wild woodland feel, as well as give you a place to sit and enjoy what you've made in the shade.

left Because trees often spring up around creeks and other water features, a pond is a natural addition to your garden, even if it has artificial origins. Water features add dimension to the garden and allow you to experiment with aquatic plants and koi, while attracting wildlife.

left The ideal woodland path material, wood chip mulch, looks at home among these shade-loving flowers. **top** Groundcovers are a good solution in large sloping wooded areas where you want to cover considerable space and control erosion. **above** Accents in wooded areas are best kept natural. This natural twig bench looks like it could have sprung up from the earth.

Region: Design for Where You Live

Deserts

The desert in bloom is a spectacular sight, but growing conditions in the desert are among the most difficult for garden plants. Fortunately, good plant selection will help you coax beauty from your desert garden. Seek out local nurseries that can advise you and supply you with the plants you need. Because desert cacti are among the most endangered species in this country, use only nursery-grown plants in your garden; don't collect plants from the wild.

Do a soil test before you begin planting to determine the pH, saline, and nutrient levels in your soil. Amend it as best you can for the plants you include. It is also advisable to determine the amount of water you have available for your garden and choose plants based on this availability.

Desert natives are some of the most interesting plants around. They include the sculptural agave family, as well as flowering perennials such as penstemon, Indian paintbrush, sage, and desert sunflowers. And, of course, there are a wide variety of cacti that can add prickly prettiness to your garden beds, borders, and containers.

Other drought-tolerant plants, such as succulents and sedums, are extremely popular. These colorful and textural plants are ideal for desert gardens as well as every other kind of garden. Plant these spiky characters in bowls or large dishes. Make sure these and all desert plants have plenty of drainage; they don't like wet roots.

The shapes and textures of arid plants are often dramatic. And they mix well with landscaping elements such as interesting rocks, dry streambeds of stones, and wood twisted by the wind. Bold colors also define desert gardens—choose accessories that add brilliant splashes of color to your landscape.

You can also add cooling touches of water. A fountain or similar water element is a staple of Spanish gardens.

opposite Desert gardens offer a wide range of color and texture.
above right Pools demand lots of water, but there's no substitute for their cooling, oasislike effect in a desert garden. *right* Thirsty plants, such as agave and echeveria, are good choices for desert gardens.

Region: Design for Where You Live

Mountains

Changes in elevation can be as dramatic to a plant community as changes in latitude. At the top of many mountains, only hardy alpine plants can withstand the cold and wind. However, a landscape full of colorful low-growing alpine plants, such as blue gentian, saxifrage, and cerastium, can make a beautiful mountain-style garden anywhere.

But there are types of gardening conditions in mountain regions other than alpine. Hot and cold temperatures, high elevations, and drying winds are some conditions that gardeners in the Mountain West and High Plains contend with. Choosing native plants suited to the weather extremes and tough conditions of these regions will ensure a more successful garden.

A rock garden on a slope is the perfect setting for plants. The rocks themselves are often as beautiful as the plants that cascade over them. Plant small varieties between the rocks, larger spreading shrubs at the base of the garden, and trailing plants at the top.

Sedums are another good choice for rock gardens in the mountains. There are dozens of selections of low-growing sedums to choose from, in a wide variety of colors and leaf shapes. Plus, they generally flower in late summer or fall, providing color when your garden needs it the most.

A rock garden is also a good setting for a water feature, whether it's a small pool or running water that simulates a fast-moving mountain stream, created by using a recirculating pump. The sound of water tumbling over rocks adds beautiful music to a mountain garden. Another natural benefit to a water source is that it attracts wildlife such as songbirds that will drink and bathe in shallow water.

above left Tame a steep slope with stairs of stone or wood ties and a multilevel sitting area. Railings made from birch saplings have a distinctively primitive mountain look. ***left*** A gentle slope turns into a mountainside when it's covered with plenty of small boulders and low-growing plants that thrive in well-drained conditions. ***opposite*** A view this spectacular hardly needs embellishment. The low-growing gardens edging the patio offer a little color and texture without competing with the view.

Style
Pick Your Look

Explore your personal style to see whether you lean more toward formal or informal, then create a garden just right for you.

Gertrude Jekyll, the revered English landscape designer and garden writer, said that a garden must fit its master every bit as well as his clothes. She knew that just as you would never wear a jacket that is too loud and splashy (or too dull and conservative) for your taste, you should never fall into a garden style unless it fits your personality like a glove.

Although there are rules of thumb about choosing a garden style, for the most part your choices depend on your personal likes and dislikes. That would seem obvious, but in matters of gardening, we can be a little like a developing adolescent, unsure and unable to articulate exactly what reflects our innermost selves.

One of the first and most important questions you should ask yourself when choosing a landscape style is: "formal or informal?" Nearly all other garden decisions will be influenced by your answer.

It used to be that formal gardens were called French and informal gardens, English. French gardens conjured up images of a mini Versailles, replete with intricate boxwood knot gardens and colored-gravel paths. English gardens meant blowsy borders, full of tumbling roses and perennials.

Few of us want either extreme. Instead, most gardens tend to be a combination of formal and informal. We may want lots of perennials merrily interweaving with one another, but we'll put them in neat rectangular beds edged in bricks.

Both styles offer inspiration in creating a garden that suits your personal style, whether it be formal, informal, or an eclectic blend of the two.

opposite This formal garden's centerpiece is the boxwood-outlined parterre, a formal element divided into four parts. A fountain placed on the central axis with equal-spaced pots contributes to the formal design. However, a few informal elements, such as the rough stone rim on the fountain and the informal pool area to the right, loosen up a garden that otherwise could be a little staid. **right** Cottage gardens can be either formal or informal, but this one is decidedly informal. Curving beds, the asymmetrically placed arbor, the winding flagstone path—all are casual.

Style: Pick Your Look

Formal landscape

Specific garden elements are immediately recognized as formal. These include geometrically shaped planting beds (usually filled with bedding plants that are changed two or three times a year), clipped hedges, topiaries (plants trained and pruned to a particular shape), straight walkways, stone walls or an element of enclosure, a central focal point, and a lawn—all laid out according to a grid and usually with an axis running down the exact center.

Formal landscapes are neat, orderly, and elegant. They are easy to design because they are symmetrical. But a formal garden can be labor intensive. For example, one of the hallmarks of a formal garden is clipped hedges—depending on their size and scale, these can take hours to trim just once, and you have to do it several times a year. But there are many ways to create formal landscapes that don't require a lot of work. Time-saving mulching techniques can cut down on weeding. And adding perennials (plants that come back every year) will mean less planting in spring. Plus, walkways of stone or brick require little care.

Contrary to popular opinion, formal gardens are not restricted to the landscapes of grand mansions. A formal garden can look just as charming outside a log cabin as it can outside a Colonial home. It's all a matter of scale and materials. Although there are classic formal plantings, you can plant outside the box, so to speak. For example, outline a parterre (small geometric garden) with herbs rather than traditional boxwood. To add color, you can include seasonal plants, such as flowering bulbs in spring, annuals in summer, and autumn-blooming perennials in fall inside the parterre.

opposite Formal gardens nearly always have an element of repetition. In this garden, it's the unusual arbors echoing each other across the axis of the formal garden that lies between them. **above right** Even rustic buildings can be at home with a formal garden design. An orderly series of rectangular beds holds herbs and flowers for cutting. They also are ideal as nursery beds, or areas filled with top-quality soil for planting seeds or nurturing cuttings and small perennials. **right** Knot gardens have a long, noble history. They are common elements in formal landscapes.

Style: Pick Your Look

Informal garden

Informal gardens have a lot of benefits, chief among them that they are forgiving. If we forget to weed and water for a while, an informal garden hides our sins much in the same way a patterned rug doesn't show a stain or two.

And for the earthy, organic types among us, a garden closer to what nature would create is most appealing. It's also a garden with few pretensions, making it a logical choice next to a small or rustic house.

Perhaps the least formal landscape is a wildflower meadow—a sunny, open area in which wildflowers and grasses are grown together, allowed to go to seed, and cut or mowed once a year. Although it sounds romantic, the reality of a meadow is that is looks unkempt much of the time, a fact you should consider before you dig up your lawn to plant wildflowers. It is not for everyone, nor for every situation. To look good, it needs space. In urban areas, it may be a hard sell to neighbors.

The idea of the meadow can be incorporated into a more traditional landscape by planting small pocket meadows—essentially large flowerbeds planted with a mixture of wildflowers and native grasses.

Wooded areas are another type of informal garden. A wooded area, which can be simply a cluster of large trees on a small lot, is perhaps one of the easiest types of informal landscapes to maintain. And just because it's shady doesn't mean that it lacks color and excitement. Adding a walkway, such as a wood-chip path, through the woods offers a sense of structure and will make it easier to enjoy the area. Shade-loving plants used in strategic places can add splashes of color and greatly enhance the beauty of even the most naturalized area.

One of the most popular forms of an informal garden includes wide (at least 4 feet) curving flowerbeds that follow no particular pattern. They're a delightful way to mix flowering shrubs, bulbs, perennials, annuals, evergreens, and even small trees in a small space. The downside is that they can become too much of a good thing and look unstructured in a negative way.

left There's a fine line between informal and wild. This garden keeps things in line with a well-cared-for clipped lawn and a bench to give a little structure. **opposite** A wildflower garden doesn't always need a meadow. Sunny front yards are ideal spots to create the most informal of gardens.

Style: Pick Your Look

Mix it up

Some of the most successful (and beautiful) gardens include elements of both formal and informal styles. Formal elements, including a lawn, can be included in a casual garden, adding a bit of elegance and style. And a casual bed within a formal garden can also add a bit of whimsy to an otherwise staid design.

Separate styles

Traditionally, in landscapes that combine formal and informal elements, the more formal areas are found close to the house. You might, for example, want to clip and prune the hedges right outside your back door or have a brick walkway that leads from the door to the focal point in the garden. For contrast, you could plant wildflowers or native plants toward the back of the property so they (with their inevitable imperfections) are seen only at a distance, where you can thoroughly enjoy their colors and textures. Or you could select rangy flowering shrubs, such as lilacs, to grow and bloom at will, without the required clipping that a boxwood hedge might need.

No matter where you land on the formal-informal scale, you'll find your garden evolving with your tastes. Gardens tend to reflect their owners' style, which tends to change over time. The gardener who at age 20 starts out with a wildflower meadow, at 60 may have transformed it into a maze of boxwood, complete with a tiered fountain in the center. So get out the spade and get growing. It's the ultimate way to find out what garden style is best for you.

opposite left Water gardens can be formal too. This one is a mossy series of rectangles and low falls. Its formal design is especially striking because it is in an informal woodland garden filled with naturalistic plantings. **opposite, top right** Even in rolling countryside, a formal garden can look right at home. This one is defined by a rustic fence to help it fit into the rural scene. **opposite, center right** An arbor adds structure and geometry to a garden that otherwise would be informal. **opposite right** Vegetable gardens especially benefit from a formal layout. Because they spend so much of the growing season in informal disarray as gardeners plant, tear up, and replant, a disciplined design adds order.

AN INFORMALLY FORMAL QUIZ

Give yourself 5 points for each of the following statements with which you agree.

AGREE

1. I love looking at a clean, neat room with everything in place. ☐

2. I wouldn't mind if someone came up with gardening-by-number, where I just could spent hours repeating the same task to achieve a certain effect. ☐

3. When I doodle, my scribbles have a lot of right angles in them. ☐

4. In my home, I tend to have a lot of stripes, squares, and other geometric patterns. ☐

5. I think a tux looks great. ☐

Give yourself 1 point for each of the next statements with which you agree.

6. I hate labor-intensive hairstyles. ☐

7. I like a garden with a lot of wild, hidden places. ☐

8. My dream garden is nothing but curving beds full of perennials and vines. ☐

9. I don't mind having a desk that's on the messy side. ☐

10. I think people should work with nature rather than try to control it. ☐

TOTAL POINTS ☐

5–10: Head for the library and read up on everything you can get your hands on about English landscape gardening. You're a gardener who loves the wild, romantic look.

11–15: Definitely work in many curving beds, and don't worry about defining a garden axis. But you can't tolerate a garden that looks unkempt, so proceed with caution.

16–20: You like a little structure, but don't overdo it. Start out with a nice, small formal herb garden and see how it goes.

21–30: Start saving up for the boxwood hedge of your dreams. And don't forget the marble chips.

Lawn
Turf Considerations

The grass will be greener on your side of the fence if you follow these simple, sensible hints for creating the yard of your dreams.

A familiar sound each weekend in neighborhoods around the country is the chorus of mowers trimming and taming their respective lawns. There's something about the achievement of the American dream that is represented by a thick, well-manicured carpet of green.

Chances are you have dreamed of having that perfect lawn, only to be rudely awakened when you wander around your yard and see imperfections: the occasional bare spots, brown patches, happy yellow dandelion heads, and invasions of creeping Charlie. Take heart! There is no mystery to achieving the perfect lawn. With the right grass type for your yard, the proper preparation, and a schedule of mowing and watering, you, too, can enjoy the lawn of your longing.

Starting with the right grass

Whether you're starting a new lawn or reviving an existing one, it helps to approach the cultivation of grass the way you would any other plant. In fact, a lawn is a garden of just one plant, made up of thousands or millions of individual grass plants—as many as 850 plants per square foot. All grasses may look more or less the same from far away, but different types of turf have different levels of insect and disease resistance; drought, shade, and foot-traffic tolerance; as well as temperature hardiness.

A lawn usually contains a combination of many grass types. Picking the right mixture for the conditions in your yard is essential. Just as a plant that thrives in dry soil will likely die in a boggy spot, an out-of-place grass will grow poorly or not at all. For example, cool-season grasses prefer a temperature range of 60–75°F and generally require less water, but summer heat can stress them. Warm-season grasses thrive in higher temperatures (80–95°F), but they lose their color when the mercury drops. However, warm-season grasses typically have deeper roots and can tolerate close mowing and heavy foot traffic.

After you've picked the right grass, you have to decide how to plant it. As with other annuals and perennials, you can start grass from seed or put live plants in the ground. With grass, that means sod. Sod is the quickest, easiest way to start a new lawn—but usually the most expensive. Sod yields a usable lawn in a few weeks. You might be able to lay a section of sod yourself, but large jobs probably demand professional installation. Grass seed is generally much cheaper than sod and can be sown by a do-it-yourselfer. However, it requires extensive preparation, good timing, and attentive follow-up care. You'll need patience, too, because seeded lawns can take months to establish. Plus, some grasses just don't start well from seed, leaving sod or plugs—small chunks of sod "plugged" into the ground—as your only options.

Understanding soil

Whether you sod or seed, your soil must be grass-friendly: deep, friable (crumbly), fertile, and well-draining. If the ground is seriously lacking in these requirements, fix the problems before you put in your new lawn. Build up shallow soil with a few inches of weed-free topsoil. Improve friability and fertility by working in compost, manure, or other organic matter. Solve drainage problems by changing the grade of your yard or installing a subsurface drainage system.

Less expensive drainage solutions include simple swales, baffles, and contours. Swales are long, narrow, shallow depressions that divert runoff. Baffles are small pieces of edging buried partly in the ground to slow runoff and let water soak in. Contours are ripples or bumps in the ground that intercept water and divert it through perforated pipe laid just under the surface.

Lawns love water like children love toys, but you can spoil both by giving them what they want too often. New lawns require more water than established ones, but too much is hazardous to

opposite A well-maintained lawn sets a tidy tone for your landscape and adds to your home's property value. It helps the environment by providing oxygen, preventing erosion, and filtering contaminants from rainwater.

left Even in rather dry climates, you can keep a small amount of lawn lush by watering with care. **top** Some shaded areas around a home benefit from plantings other than lawn. **above** Grass can be used for more than a big expanse of lawn. Here, turf is a living ribbon to lead visitors in and out of the garden.

Lawn: Turf Considerations

any lawn's health. Overwatering keeps the top layer of soil wet, encouraging grass to develop weak, shallow roots, the kind that lead to quick injury in hot, dry weather. Infrequent but deep watering provides the best results.

Feeding your lawn

Lawns need to be fed as well as watered, but the diet must be strict. Overfertilizing can be as harmful as overwatering. Too much fertilizer leaves plants weak and top-heavy, making them perfect targets for disease and insects. Fertilize only if a soil test reveals a deficiency. Otherwise, if you must give your lawn a snack, it makes sense to fertilize only during growth spurts in the spring and fall.

The type of fertilizer you choose and when you apply it depend on the type of grass. Most commercial fertilizers are a combination of nitrogen, phosphorus, and potassium. Of these ingredients, the most important for grass is nitrogen, which promotes leaf growth and good color. You already have an excellent source of nitrogen—grass clippings. Leaving clippings on the lawn is a cheap, easy way to fertilize.

Despite your best efforts to keep your lawn well fed and healthy, it still may fall victim to weeds. Any weed can be removed by hand, but if you don't get the whole plant, you'll find yourself bending and pulling again and again. Weeds over a large area may demand a chemical solution.

If you had a weed problem last year, apply an herbicide in early spring. A pre-emergent control can wipe out crabgrass by killing the young plants as they sprout. Another application in late spring can help control dandelions and other broadleaf (nongrass) weeds. To save time, weed and feed simultaneously by applying a combination herbicide and fertilizer. If you're cautious about chemicals, soap herbicides are less toxic than other types. Don't broadly apply any herbicide in summer, when your lawn is most stressed by heat.

If all this feeding and weeding sounds a little daunting, there's no shame in checking into a lawn service. Call around and price their services, then compare what you would pay for lawn products applied yourself. You may find that the costs are similar.

WATER WISDOM

Unless your yard is somehow blessed with perfectly timed rainfall throughout the growing season, you'll need to supplement nature's water supply with your own. Here are some tips for watering grass wisely.

- Water heavily at infrequent intervals. On average, a lawn needs about 1 inch of water per week, either from rainfall or irrigation. This will soak the soil to a depth of 4–6 inches, putting water deep into your lawn's root system. Let the lawn dry out completely between intervals. Place small cans around the yard to measure how fast your system delivers water and to ensure uniform coverage. A thorough watering takes awhile, however, so be prepared to leave your water source on for several hours.

- The best times to water are early morning or early evening, when there is generally less wind and heat. Cool, calm conditions limit evaporation, allow greater soil penetration, and reduce runoff.

- Most watering systems apply water faster than the lawn can soak it in. Pause your watering when puddles or runoff occur, and let water penetrate the soil before resuming. Water soaks in at different speeds in different soil types. If you have extremely sandy soil, it could take as little as a half-hour for an inch of water to soak in. With clay, it could take 10 times longer—about five hours—for an inch of water to soak in.

- Keep a newly seeded lawn moist but not soaked during the germination process. Too much water can cause poor germination and disease. A light mulch over the seed will help keep the soil moist. As the new lawn grows, reduce the frequency of watering and increase the amount applied. After four to six weeks, treat the new lawn as an established one.

- For a newly sodded lawn, soak it completely for about two weeks after placement, watering every day or two. This will allow the root system to become firmly established.

Lawn: Turf Considerations

Mowing rules

If your grass is growing, you'll be mowing. You probably like to keep your hair at a certain length with regular trims, and that's what grass likes too. Each grass type looks best and stays healthiest at a certain height. Use your mower to maintain that height as closely as possible. Giving your lawn a too-short crew cut can be just as damaging as letting the grass grow to hippie length. The basic rule of mowing is to never cut more than one-third of the leaf blade. If this works out to mowing every Saturday, great. However, weather and growth spurts may require adjusting your schedule. Despite what your dad might have said, it's OK to mow your lawn a second time during the week.

It's also important not to scalp your lawn, a common sin. In the cooler weather of spring and fall, grasses should be cut at 2–2½ inches. When temperatures start topping 80 degrees, let the grass get taller—as much as 3½ inches for bluegrass. It won't have the same perfect appearance as a lawn cut shorter, but it will more than make up for style in plant health. Taller blades shade the soil, conserving moisture and preventing weed seeds from germinating.

The right grass, good soil, and timely care should have you well on the way to a champion lawn. Be patient—a lawn, like the other living parts of your landscape, takes several seasons to mature and fill in completely. When it does, don't be surprised to catch a few neighbors admiring your lawn and wondering what your secret is.

THE GREEN STUFF

All grass may look alike, but a beautiful lawn usually contains a combination of distinct grass types, each with its own strengths and weaknesses. If you want a healthy, attractive lawn, the mixture you choose must fit the growing conditions around your home: climate, sun and shade exposure, and amount of foot traffic. Plus, you want a grass with an appearance—height, texture, and color—in keeping with your overall landscape. Most grass manufacturers package grass combinations to make your choice easier.

TYPE OF GRASS	SEASON	TEXTURE	GERMINATION	SHADE TOLERANCE	DROUGHT TOLERANCE	TRAFFIC RESISTANCE	OPTIMUM HEIGHT	OTHER
Kentucky bluegrass	Cool	Fine	Slow	Fair	Fair	Good	2–3½ inches	Goes dormant during drought and winter
Perennial ryegrass	Cool	Medium-coarse	Fast	Good	Good	Excellent	1½–2½ inches	Poor tolerance of temperature extremes and winter
Fine fescue	Cool	Fine	Medium-slow	Excellent	Excellent	Fair	1½–2½ inches	Loses color in drought; may spread undesirably
Turf-type tall fescue	Cool/warm	Medium-coarse	Medium-slow	Excellent	Good	Excellent	2½–3½ inches	May appear clumpy
Zoysia grass	Cool/warm	Fine-medium	Slow—use plugs or sod	Good	Good	Good	1–2 inches	Turns brown in winter
Buffalo grass	Warm	Fine	Medium—use plugs	Poor	Excellent	Excellent	2 inches	Tolerates alkaline soil; turns brown midsummer; grows no more than 4–6 inches
Bermuda grass	Warm	Fine	Slow—use plugs or sod	Poor	Excellent	Excellent	1–2 inches	May be too aggressive
Centipede grass	Warm	Medium-coarse	Medium—use plugs or sod	Good	Good	Poor	1½–2½ inches	Grows no more than 4-6 inches
St. Augustine grass	Warm	Coarse	Slow—use plugs or sod	Excellent	Poor	Fair	2–3 inches	Very poor cold tolerance; susceptible to disease

Light
Sun vs. Shade

Choose plants for your landscape based on how much sunlight your yard receives.

One of the biggest influences in choosing the plants you'll grow is how much sunlight your yard receives. For example, the majority of perennials thrive in six hours of sun, but thanks to the many plants that unfurl fabulous foliage and beautiful blooms in less light, you can plan a striking garden even in shady conditions.

Inventory sunlight

Gauge how much sunlight bathes your garden site. It's best to assess light patterns every hour or two in the course of a day, noting where shadows fall, linger, and pass. If you spy sunlight trails during spring, bare-branch trees often give the illusion of sunny spots beneath; what you think is a sunny area might be swallowed by shade when leaves emerge. Buildings and walls also cast shadows; consider those structures as you plot the sun's path.

Use marking flags and spray paint to indicate light and shadow in your yard, or create a light map on paper. Start with a few sheets of tracing paper, sketching a copy of your yard's outline on each page. About two hours after sunrise, observe where light and shade fall and mark them on the tracing paper, noting the time. Repeat the process through the day, each time using a different sheet of paper. Stop recording about an hour before dusk. Use a pencil to mark shady sections of the yard on each page. Label sun and shade pockets to indicate whether they reflect morning or afternoon conditions. Layer the pages together, and you'll get an accurate picture of how much light your yard receives. Create a composite drawing to use as a one-page light map.

No hard-and-fast rules

Once you know your garden site's sun and shade characteristics, start choosing perennials. A plant's light needs are more fluid than static. For instance, if you plant a sun-loving plant in a shade-dappled spot, you won't necessarily kill it, but you'll likely experience fewer flowers, shorter life span, less color, or gangly stems.

opposite Gardens planted beneath trees often boast a blend of sun and shade. Study sunlight patterns throughout the day and during various seasons, then slip sun-loving perennials into sunny pockets.

THE FACTS OF LIGHT

As you read about specific plants, you'll find that each plant has its own light requirements: full sun, part sun, part shade, or full shade. Unsure what these terms mean? You're not alone. Here's how to decipher the light code.

FULL SUN: Plants require at least 6 hours of sun per day.

PART SUN: Plants should receive 3 to 6 hours of sun per day, preferably in morning or evening, not during the hottest parts of the day.

PART SHADE: Plants will thrive with 3 to 6 hours of sun per day, but definitely require shade during the afternoon, when the sun is hottest.

FULL SHADE: Plants need fewer than 3 hours of direct sun per day. Filtered sunlight or light shade is necessary for the rest of the day.

Regional influences

A plant's light requirements shift throughout the United States. In the South, sun-loving perennials might need shade during the hottest part of the day, while in the Pacific Northwest, cloud cover can prevent sun-lovers from flourishing. Where cool, wet summers prevail, perennials that nominally prefer partial shade can thrive in sunnier conditions.

Light: Sun vs. Shade

Understanding sunlight is simple: A plant receives sun or it does not. The intensity of sunlight varies based on time of day, with morning light offering softer, gentler rays and afternoon sun blazing with sizzling rays.

Shade presents a more complex scenario, full of nuances and degrees. There's the deep shade you find on the north side of a house; alongside a stone wall or privacy fence; or beneath a 70-year-old beech tree, where the sun only peeps through from winter through early spring. Dappled shade dances beneath honey locust trees, where small leaves filter sunlight.

Deciduous trees offer seasonal shade. Spring sunlight under leafless boughs provides the perfect footing for ephemeral plants, such as bleeding heart or wood anemone, which stage an early-season flower show and then quietly disappear as leaves emerge and shade deepens. As the sun heads north for summer in the Northern hemisphere, shade patterns shift and shorten, then silently lengthen as summer slips into fall. Observe seasonal light patterns as you choose and situate plants for your landscape.

Shade, shade, go away

You can make some shade do a disappearing act. If you have a tree with branches that cast dense shade, lighten the scenery below by removing lower limbs. This process, called limbing up, effectively lifts a canopy, permitting sunlight to penetrate the leafy shade. During late summer and fall, sunlight can slant beneath limbed-up trees to lighten deep shade. Selectively thinning can increase light to the ground below. Consider replacing solid fences with vine-covered lattice to increase light.

Dealing with dry shade

Dry shade under mature trees is one of a garden's toughest conditions, but perennials can splash color into these droughty, dark areas. For plants to thrive until they're established, they'll need frequent watering. Plants will deliver a modest flower show that slowly increases over time.

left In a woodland setting, tall trees often cast light shade punctuated by shafts of sunlight. Count on reliable shade performers such as astilbe to brighten shady gardens with colorful blossom spires. Plant a mix of astilbe that bloom at different points in the season to create a long-lasting flower show. Planting companions for astilbe include golden hakonegrass, goatsbeard, and ferns.

above Sometimes shade comes from structures such as buildings or fences. In these cases, you might deal with heavy shade that lingers for part of the day until the sun shifts.

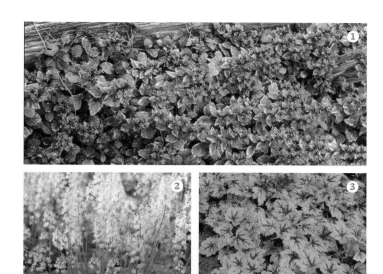

FLOWERS AND FOLIAGE FOR SHADE

Different perennials perform in varying degrees of shade. Generally, plants that thrive in deep shade, such as these perennials, will also prosper in part shade. Try some of these flower and foliage favorites to pump up the beauty in shady corners of your yard.

1. BUGLEWEED Mat-forming groundcover with blue flowers in spring; foliage in various hues—bronze, rose, white, green, or purple. Zones 4–10.

2. FOAMFLOWER Groundcover with white or pink blooms in mid-spring; evergreen in warm climates. Zones 3–9.

3. FOAMY BELLS Groundcover with cut leaves in an array of hues and variegation patterns; white, cream, or pink blooms in spring. Zones 5–8.

4. HEART-LEAF BERGENIA Shiny evergreen leaves and pink spring blooms; deer-resistant. Zones 4–10.

5. HOSTA Foliage plant in an array of hues and variegations. Zones 3-9.

6. JACOB'S LADDER Blue, white, or pink blooms in spring; variegated leaf forms brighten shade. Zones 4–9.

7. LUNGWORT Silver- or white-speckled, deep green leaves; some forms feature greater leaf variegation. Zones 2–8.

8. ROSE TURTLEHEAD Upright, clumping plant with pink to white flower spikes in late summer and fall. Zones 4–9.

9. VARIEGATED SOLOMON'S SEAL Arching stems hold cream-edge leaves that turn gold in fall. Zones 4–9.

10. YELLOW CORYDALIS Yellow blooms dangle above lacy foliage from spring through fall. Zones 5–8.

CHAPTER TWO

Structural Elements

Discover the creative building blocks of a landscape that make it useful and beautiful.

From Here to There
Walkways

Every landscape needs a way to move from one place to another.

A walk is the usual route from the street or parking area to the front door. It creates a first impression and sets the tone for the house and garden. Comfort, safety, and a clear choice of direction are the three hallmarks of a well-designed walk.

A walk is generally more formal than a garden path. As a rule, a walk is at least 3 feet wide and rarely more than 4 feet wide—enough so two adults can stroll comfortably side-by-side without either of them running into plant material adjacent to the walk at ground or shoulder level.

For safety, a walk needs to be well-lit, level, and made of a firm material that is not slippery when wet. Materials to avoid include gravel, which can be difficult to walk on, and glazed ceramic tile, which can be slick when wet.

The walk should be obvious to visitors. The direction of the walk and its destination should be easily visible—whether the walk begins at the street, driveway, sidewalk, or parking area.

Plot the purpose

Although the primary purpose of most walks is to lead the way to the front door, a walk can also be the route from the parking area to another entrance of the house. A walk can ensure easy access between the house and heavily trafficked areas of the garden, such as a swimming pool or terrace.

In the garden, a walk is the route that wheelbarrows and garden carts can traverse. The width and firm surface make it easy to transport heavy loads of soil, compost, or tools and supplies between a compost bin or garden shed and the vegetable or flower garden.

opposite A meandering brick path leads through a garden to a gate. It looks inviting and romantic. **above right** The stone in this walk echoes the stone in the wall, unifying the whole area. Crisp edging along the walk simplifies lawn chores. **right** Make a long, straight walk exciting by flanking it with a multilevel planting bed. Add interest by edging the walk with a contrasting material.

From Here to There: Walkways

Choose a walkway style

A walk can be either straight or curving. Because most walks begin or terminate at the house, the design style should fit the architecture. The material you use to build the walk is a matter of style.

A straight walk appears more formal than a curved walk. It is a no-nonsense means to get you directly to a destination, and it is less expensive and easier to build than a curved walk.

A gently curving walk lends itself to less formal settings. It is appropriate only when there is enough room for gentle, sweeping arcs. When there is only a short distance to travel—20 feet or less—curving a walkway results in small, tight arcs that are too angular for comfortable walking.

A walk creates a transition from one area to another, so it's important to think about the experience people will have as they move along it. A straight course through an expanse of lawn is not very exciting; a walk that passes beneath an arbor, near ornamental trees, or along a flowerbed is more enjoyable. The placement of the walk should take into account the views approaching the house and those leading away.

Proportion is an important consideration. A short, straight walk of 20 feet or less rarely needs to be more than 3 feet wide. Longer, curving walks can be 4 feet wide, or may be made to appear wider when flanked with an undulating 3- to 4-foot-wide flowerbed.

Plants alongside a walk often feel and look right at about 3 feet tall. Taller plants can evoke a closed-in feeling, and they require more maintenance to keep them pruned out of the way.

above left A gently curving walk creates an attractive entryway to a front door. *left* Large concrete pavers set in a bed of gravel create a comfortable yet formal walk from a parking area to a patio.

From Here to There
Paths

A path is a leisurely route that guides people through a garden, putting them in close contact with plants and other landscape features.

A path may not connect with the house or even be visible from it. Unlike a walk, the design and materials of a path can be a reflection of the garden rather than the style of the house. Using path materials that complement adjacent features in the landscape allows the path to blend with its surroundings and create a harmonious setting.

Why have a garden path?

Practicality often dictates the creation of a path. A practical path defines a route that people walk routinely. Look for trodden footpaths in the grass; these are "desire lines" that show where a path should be laid. If you have an existing path that nobody uses, remove it and locate a path where it will be used.

Install a practical path even if the need is occasional. For example, if you drag hoses to a specific part of the garden several times a week, a path will make the chore easier. Use hose guards around any curves in a path to protect the plants. Use the path to direct guests from the garden to the back door or to special areas within the garden.

A path can be an art form; consider it horizontal sculpture. Whether it's a strong, sweeping line or a gentle curve that meanders through a series of beds, a path leads the eye. When you lay out a path, think about where it will lead and what people will see as they stroll along it. The choice of paving material itself can contribute to a pleasing appearance.

Have fun with paths. They can go anywhere you want. Dead-end a path at a shrub bed, or make one that goes in a big circle. Wind a curving path among trees and bend it out of sight. Make your path with unusual materials. Homemade stepping-stones embedded with found objects, pieces of pottery, or your family's handprints in the concrete personalize the path.

Perfect path materials

The design of a path influences the choice of material. Knowing the effects and best uses of different materials helps you select the most appropriate one.

Stone Versatile and widely used, stone is set in mortar or sand, mixed with other materials, or used alone to mark footfalls along the path. When possible, use indigenous stone, which blends with the landscape better than anything else.

Brick Second only to stone in popularity, brick is used in many homes. A brick path ties these homes and gardens together. Old brick is desirable. Its aged appearance makes any garden seem well-established. Like stone, brick can be set in sand or mortar or mixed with other materials.

Pavers Available in a range of styles, shapes, and colors, from inexpensive plain concrete squares readily found at home centers to high-end ceramic tiles, pavers have a style to fit any budget. When designing a path with pavers, experiment with pattern, especially when using small pavers (4–6 inches across). The broad choices of colors make it easy to create a woven patchwork design.

Stepping-stones A variety of stepping-stones—ready-made in many styles and sizes as well as do-it-yourself kits—is available at garden and home centers. Experiment with different materials to create your own. Two-inch-thick disks cut from the base of a felled tree set the tone for a woodland path.

Concrete stepping-stones are easy to make. Build a form from 2×2s; pour concrete into the form, let it set, then remove the form. To personalize the stepping-stones, press large leaves, coins, handprints, pottery shards, or other found objects into the concrete as it hardens.

Grass A path is a role reversal for grass; usually a path made of a solid material cuts through a lawn. A strip of grass leading through a paved or planted area can be dramatic. Design a grass path so one or two quick passes of a mower will keep it trimmed.

From Here to There: Paths

Mulch For a casual look, organic mulch is easy on the garden. It allows water to pass through to the soil below, and it slowly breaks down into nutrients. Replenish the mulch at least once a year as it decomposes. Set the edging 1–2 inches higher than the path to keep the mulch in bounds. Some types of mulch are easier to walk on than others. Bark nuggets are too coarse for comfort.

Gravel Elegant to look at and easy to work with, gravel costs less than many materials. Use it to create the appearance of a dry stream, enhanced by a few large stones along the path. If one of the purposes of your path is a peaceful place to walk, you may not like the crunching sound that gravel makes when it is walked on.

Building a path

Laying out a path is easier than laying out a walk because a path is more informal and less exact, and the width can vary along the way. Imperfection is part of the charm of a path.

A walk is designed to get you quickly and comfortably from one place to another, whereas a path can meander through the garden, letting you take your time along the way. The path can even weave among trees, shrubs, and other garden features.

Once you know the starting and ending points, you can lay out the path exactly. Walk the desired route, and mark the centerline of the path with stakes or pieces of coat-hanger wire with bright color cloth tied to one end. As you walk the route of the path, insert a marker into the ground every 5 feet. When you reach the end of the path, turn around and walk back to the beginning. Change the path if you want. Walk the path in both directions several times, and make adjustments as you go. Pay attention to the terrain; avoid steep slopes, roots, and other obstacles. Direct the path to the special features of the garden. Focus on views above eye level; take advantage of the good views and avoid the poor ones.

left Moss hugs concrete pavers, making a path that doubles as a patio for outdoor dining. ***opposite above*** Use local building materials when possible. Local stone is usually less expensive than stone shipped from far away. ***opposite left*** A grass pathway can be a beautiful way to separate two large flower beds. ***opposite middle*** Set individual stones into an existing path for a route that is both solid and water-permeable. ***opposite right*** Mulch around set-in stone to create a weed-free path.

Once you have the centerline of the path laid out, mark the side boundaries. If you are using individual stepping-stones, walk the path in your normal gait. Mark exactly where to center each stone for a comfortable pace. When placing the stones, keep in mind the stride of others using the path; arrange stones closer together for children.

A dual-purpose path

A path that doubles as a patio is a good use of limited space. Make the path at least 4 feet wide and as long as you want; avoid a long, straight line. Stagger a straight path so you don't see it all at once. The result is a large area that is ideal for outdoor entertaining yet still feels intimate.

Mixing materials on a combination path and patio allows the area to look and feel like both. Break up the paving with gravel, mulch, or low-growing herbs and groundcovers. Or set stepping-stones or pavers into an existing lawn path or other narrow strip of grass.

Materials for Walks & Paths

Brick

Before deciding on brick, remember that unless you want to cut bricks to fit, the line of the walk or path must be straight or uniformly and gently curved. Brick is a durable and refined material that is relatively expensive and time-consuming to lay. Old brick costs even more unless you find someone who is tearing down a brick structure. Most salvaged brick has clinging mortar that you have to chip away. New brick is available in a range of colors and finishes. The only potential maintenance on brick is removing a white residue (alkaline salts) that may appear; scrub the brick with a fiber brush dipped in muriatic acid.

Stone

Refined stone, such as slate or marble, is more uniform, durable, and costly than fieldstone. Fieldstone is a more forgiving medium. It is imperfect in its natural state, so slight variances from a level or straight line don't stand out. Slate, marble, and fieldstone are virtually maintenance-free. Sandstone, although attractive, has a tendency to chip, shatter, and flake from physical damage, freezing, and thawing.
Stone prices and availability vary depending on location and regional geography. Keep an eye out for renovation and construction projects; they often unearth mounds of stone that must be disposed of or sold as salvage.

Exposed aggregate

Exposed aggregate—concrete with a high percentage of uniform pea- to marble-size stones mixed in or added to the finish layer—is durable when properly installed by a professional. When the concrete is poured, the very top layer of masonry is washed or brushed off to expose the aggregate. Only 20–30 percent of the top layer of aggregate is exposed. Stone used for exposed aggregate is available in shades of brown to gray. It costs more than plain concrete but less than stamped concrete or pavers. Unless you use very coarse aggregate, this material can be slippery when wet.

Paving stones

Concrete pavers offer a wide range of colors and patterns and are relatively inexpensive. All you need to install concrete pavers is a firm, smooth base of sand and some sweat equity. Held in by sturdy edging, concrete pavers are easy to install and offer many of the virtues of concrete. Establish the width of the path by laying out a row of pavers. Choose a layout that requires minimal cutting. Your path should be at least 3 feet wide. Keep the path at least 2 feet away from trees, large bushes, and hedges.

Gravel

Gravel allows water to percolate through, so the path drains better than any other type. You will find a range of gravels to choose from; you do not need to hire a professional to make a gravel path. Crusher-run is a granite mix containing medium and small stones as well as granite dust, which helps bind the materials together. River rock and pebbles are more expensive and have a refined look. Gravel maintenance is limited to keeping the material in place and replenishing it when it gets thin.

Mixed media

Making a list of the building materials used in your hardscape and building your walk with a mix of materials on that list is a useful way to unify different materials found throughout the garden. It can be challenging to come up with a mix that looks good. Brick and concrete are a common combination; stone and concrete also work well. A stone-and-brick mixture is less common and can be hard to blend. The cost, availability, and durability of this type of path will vary with the materials used.

Mulch

Use mulch for a quick and easy path. Depending upon the availability of the mulch you choose, this can be the least expensive path to make. Durability depends on the material you use. Pine straw breaks down quickly, whereas bark nuggets take much longer to decompose but tend to feel coarse underfoot. Maintenance is limited; keep the mulch within the desired boundaries, and replenish the mulch as required. Edging defines the path and keeps the mulch in place. Mulch is not recommended for a path that needs to handle a wheelbarrow or garden cart.

Stained and stamped concrete

Concrete can be more than a plain gray slab. Stained, painted, or textured concrete looks attractive. You can stain it yourself; add color to the concrete during mixing or curing. Painting is an option that requires regular touch-ups every two to three years, depending on how much the walk is used.

Stamped concrete is made by pressing a metal form into damp concrete. When it dries, a single slab of concrete looks as though it is made of many individual stones or pavers. Stamped concrete is highly durable. The tools needed to stamp concrete are cost-prohibitive for small areas.

left Paint a fence a dark color, such as green, to help it fade into the background or blend with the garden. **top** Picket fences are one of the most popular fence styles, with myriad design options. **above** A fence doesn't have to be costly. This simple and rustic fence uses small limbs from the property nailed to cross rails.

Beautiful Barriers
Fences

For beauty, visual separation, containment, and security, fences offer a wide range of uses in the landscape.

Fencing has been a part of the landscape as long as there have been gardens. Fences are multipurpose. They create security and privacy, define boundaries, keep people and animals contained, and add to the garden's aesthetics. The range of styles and materials, as well as the relative ease of building fences, adds to their appeal.

Fence uses

Security and privacy Fences used for this purpose are typically large, solid, or otherwise imposing structures. To reduce the visual weight of such a structure, add vines, a wall fountain, plaques, or other artwork. Paint a trompe l'oeil opening to give the illusion of a passageway or an airy space. Use an open-style construction to reduce the visual impact of the structure and allow light and air to pass through.

Defining space One of the original reasons for fencing land was to claim ownership. The habit is still prevalent. A fence does not have to be large to define space. A 2-foot-high fence communicates that you want people to stay out of the area.

Fences are frequently used to surround a lot for no other reason than to mark the property line. When erecting a fence for this purpose, be aware of the exact property line and any required restrictions on placement, type of fence, or height.

Use a fence instead of a solid wall to create an outdoor room. It is much less expensive than most walls. As an added advantage, a fence is usually much more readily moved or expanded than a wall as your garden grows or your design ideas or needs change.

Controlling traffic A fence—whether large or small—does a good job of directing people where you want them to go and to avoid the places where you don't want them.

If using a tall fence, think about how it will feel to walk beside it. To soften the impact of all the wood or metal, consider putting a planting bed a few feet in front of the fence or using vines on it.

Aesthetic appeal Consider all aspects and effects of a fence—appearances count a lot. Whether the pleasure is in forming a backdrop for a planting or in the beauty of the craftsmanship and design, sometimes the best reason to have a fence is simply because it is attractive.

A solid fence serves as a backdrop to whatever is in front of it. Plant a specimen tree or shrub in front of the fence, and use night lighting so it can be enjoyed at all hours. Consider how the color of the fence works with what is planted in front if it. Should you be ready for a change, it is easily accomplished by painting all or part of the fence a different color.

Fence styles

There are many styles of fences; how you use your fence will affect your choice. For example, if you want a decorative option, a picket fence is popular. If privacy is your goal, choose a solid-style fence such as a stockade. If you need to keep a dog contained, you may choose functional chain link.

Traditional A white picket fence is the most traditional type of fence and common in many areas, yet it is one of the most diverse in design. There is virtually no limit to how you space and design the pickets, posts, and rails. The classic picket fence is painted white, but other colors may better suit your scheme. Or you may choose to leave your pickets unpainted and natural. A stockade fence is another option. This type of fence is made of panels of 1×8-inch pieces of wood placed shoulder to shoulder. Both picket and stockade fences are easy to build. Most home centers sell precut components or prefabricated panels.

Formal or informal The most formal fences are made of wrought iron. They tend to be expensive and add an elegant look to a home. Informal fences include split-rail, lattice, bamboo, and woven wood, which work best in rural or wooded gardens. Funky, fun, or folk art fences also fit this category.

Functional Chain link is durable, affordable, and easy to install. It lets air and light pass through and can be made any height. It also comes in dark colors that blend with the landscape.

Fence materials

With the purpose and style of your fence in mind, the next step is to determine the appropriate material. As you decide, be aware of the maintenance that each type of fence requires.

Wood This material is the most affordable, available, and versatile for fencing. It comes in uniform sizes, so you can easily plan, purchase, and build the fence yourself. Prefabricated wood

Beautiful Barriers: Fences

fence panels are available at most home centers. Use naturally rot-resistant wood species such as redwood or cedar, or use treated lumber.

Some wood fences are made from unfinished wood. Split-rail fences and log fences can be made from store-bought posts and rails or from materials found on your property. Making a fence is a good way to recycle deadwood or wood from storm-ravaged or downed trees. The longevity of the fence depends on the wood used and your climate. As a rule, a fence made from fallen timber will last about half as long as one made from rot-resistant or treated lumber.

Metal Wrought iron implies permanence, order, and wealth. Historically, metal fences were custom-made of wrought iron. Because of the relatively low demand for it, wrought iron is now fairly hard to find. Estate sales are a good source.

The quality and pricing of aluminum fences make them an attractive alternative to iron. Aluminum fences come in a wide range of styles. They are easy to work with and lightweight. Aluminum fences do not rot or rust, so the paint lasts longer than on wood or iron.

Combination fences A fence can be made of more than one type of material. For example, masonry pillars instead of posts, with metal or wooden panels in between, achieve some of the permanence and elegance of stone without the massive feel of a solid wall. Coupling rustic posts with finished panels is a good way to tie together various aspects of the garden through building materials.

Freestyle This is a catchall category for unusual fences that don't fit any other description. Usually reserved for the bold and adventurous homeowner, a freestyle fence can be made from almost any materials—metal car bumpers, old highway signs, vertical cross ties, bedsprings. A freestyle fence serves all the functions of a traditional fence while revealing more of the owner's character.

top left A fence defines the boundaries of the garden and serves as a backdrop. Notice how this fence blends with the plantings to become part of the design. **above left** A metal fence combined with ornate concrete pillars is stately and elegant. Its austerity is tempered by the playful blue paint. **left** Fences can feature more than one design element, such as a solid-board fence topped with lattice.

Fence maintenance

The type and amount of maintenance a fence requires is based mostly on the material used to build it.

The combination of wood, paint, and weather conditions necessitates repainting a wood fence every four to five years. It may be necessary to do some touch-up painting between complete paint jobs. If you use a rot-resistant wood or treated lumber, you can prolong the life of the fence by applying a sealer or stain at the time of construction and prior to painting.

Any wood fence will last longer if you keep it clean. Spray it with a strong blast from a hose to wash away decaying leaves or other vegetation nestled in corners.

Training a vine to climb a fence can create an ideal condition for decay due to trapped debris, blocked light, lack of air circulation, and moisture retention. A vine-covered fence is difficult to paint. When it becomes necessary to repaint, gently remove the vine and lower it to the ground, paint the fence, then reattach and retrain the vine. In some cases, it is easier to cut back the vine to within a foot or more of the ground and allow it to regrow on the fence.

The only maintenance needed for a metal fence is occasional painting. When repainting metal (or wood, for that matter), it is best to scrape off all the old paint, remove the rust, and prime the metal before applying more paint.

DRESS UP WITH VINES

Wrought-iron fences lend an air of permanence to the garden. Maintenance is limited to rust removal and painting. Annual vines such as morning glory, cup-and-saucer vine, and hyacinth bean vine look lovely on an iron fence and die back when frost comes.

Fence Finishes

1. NATURAL WOOD
- Letting a fence age naturally is inexpensive and trouble-free.
- A natural fence blends well with informal or rustic surroundings.
- Even rot-resistant woods, such as redwood, cedar, or treated pine, will fade to gray over time. Adding a stain or a sealer will prolong its life and natural color.

2. PAINT
- You can use any color of outdoor paint.
- A dark-color fence seems to recede.
- Be sure the wood is completely dry before painting; otherwise, the paint will bubble as moisture escapes.
- Remove cracked or peeling paint before repainting.
- Always use a primer when painting a metal fence.
- Use a sprayer instead of a brush to save time.

3. STAIN
- A sealer or stain prolongs the life of the wood.
- Stain gives a natural look. Clear-stained wood ages to the same color as untreated wood.
- A stain can make one wood species look like another.
- Stain is thinner than paint. Apply stain liberally so the wood can soak it up.
- Brushes work better than sprayers.

4. NATURAL IRON
- Iron fencing is long lasting and comes in a wide variety of heights and design types.
- Iron fencing can be coated, painted, or left to rust. Rusted fences are popular in cottage gardens.

Beautiful Barriers
Walls

Walls project a sense of permanence and, if built right, should last a lifetime.

A wall serves the same purpose as a fence. It provides privacy and security, and it defines spaces. A wall also creates a mood in a garden. There are three main ways to categorize walls: by type, by size, and by material. Because of the expense and scale of walls, plan carefully before building. Your choice of wall type will be based on a combination of use, home and garden style, and budget.

Wall options

Wall size and shape vary based primarily upon use. Security and privacy walls need to be 6–8 feet tall. A wall this size requires substantial footings and takes up a lot of space.

If you're building such a wall for security reasons, consider using a lattice-style brick design, which leaves open spaces for light and air to move through. You can do this only when using brick or cinder block because stone and poured concrete do not readily lend themselves to this construction. You can add strength to this type of wall by giving it a serpentine or undulating shape to add tremendous visual interest as well.

A large solid expanse can be a little daunting, so consider painting a mural on the wall, adding a window with shutters, or creating a mosaic. A wall also lends itself to having a tree, shrub, or vine espaliered to it or a vine growing up and over it. This is best done by planting on the sunny side of the wall and allowing the plants to drape over the top.

Another idea is to add a planter to the top of the wall. This is easy if you plan for it from the beginning, although most walls can be retrofitted to accommodate a planter. As with any container garden, a wall planter has specific and regular maintenance needs. The idea is most practical with a drip irrigation system. You will need to be able to easily and safely tend to the plants.

When it comes to large walls, the best bet is to work with a professional. There is nothing particularly hard about building a large wall, but errors could be costly, especially true in areas where the frost depth exceeds 1 foot. In Zones 5 and colder, foundation footings may need to be as deep as 4 feet, which involves moving a lot of dirt and mixing a lot of concrete.

Perhaps you need only a short wall to guide people through the garden and keep them out of certain areas. Short walls are easier for the average homeowner to build.

There are also wall-building systems, which are modular blocks designed to interlock. Most do not require mortar to hold them in place, so they can shift and heave as temperatures change and do not have the footing requirements of a wall set in mortar. As long as modular walls do not exceed 4 feet in height, they can be built by the average homeowner. Taller walls can sway, and a poorly built wall can topple.

Two materials are most commonly used to build walls: stone and masonry. Masonry includes preformed materials such as brick, cinder block, and modular wall components. Cost and appropriate style will determine which you should use.

Stone walls

Stone walls can be works of art. They instantly convey the look of an established garden. After all, stone is one of the oldest, if not the original, material used for building walls. Enhance the timeworn appearance of a stone wall with a covering of moss.

When considering a stone wall, it is important to know what materials are available locally. This is helpful in choosing a style that fits your setting. It also helps in reducing the cost of the wall. Stone is heavy and expensive to ship, so using local materials will usually cost less.

Most tall stone walls (more than 3–4 feet) are held in place by mortar and rest on a concrete footing just like a masonry wall. This is true whether the wall is made of solid rock or masonry faced with stone.

Large solid-stone walls require a great amount of experience and time to create. They may be best left to an experienced craftsperson. But if you want to build one yourself, consider making a smaller wall or building a cinder-block wall, then facing it with stone. This method of construction is easier and more economical, and it requires less stone.

opposite A wall can be constructed from mixed materials (such as stone and stucco) and contain decorative elements such as a fountain. *top right* Capping a long or large wall with a contrasting material is an attractive way to seal the wall. *above right* Build a wall with a contemporary look by choosing industrial materials such as galvanized sheeting. *right* A well-constructed wall made from stone is costly, but it will last for decades.

65

left This stone wall is not as hard to build as it looks. Allow plenty of time and plenty of stone, or hire it done professionally. ***top*** A brick wall creates a solid and formal backdrop. ***above*** Low walls in patio settings create a sense of enclosure without blocking the view. Plus, they are an ideal spot for adding flower containers.

Beautiful Barriers: Walls

To build such a wall, you must first prepare a footing. Check local building codes to determine the footing's required depth and width. A footing typically begins as a trench dug to the proper depth and twice the width of the finished wall, followed by wood forms that are then filled with concrete.

Build the wall to the desired height, laying ½ inch of mortar between each course of blocks. Place metal straps (called ties) about every 12 inches along the wall; they should protrude 4–6 inches on either side of the cinder block. These give the stone and the mortar used to face the wall something to hold onto.

Once the cinder-block wall is built, start attaching the stone, using liberal amounts of mortar between the wall and stone and at least ½ inch of mortar between stones.

Masonry walls

Masonry walls, whether brick, cinder block, or modular block, are relatively easy to build once you have a good footing in place. With a level footing, it's simply a matter of laying level courses.

Use sheets of fiberglass or metal mesh between courses to add strength.

Care and maintenance

You may need to remove discoloration or repair loose mortar. Efflorescence is the term for the powdery white mineral deposits that occur on brick. To remove it, wet the wall thoroughly with a strong blast from a garden hose, then use a stiff-bristle brush to scrub off the deposits. (A wire brush will scrape the brick.) Remove recurring deposits by scrubbing with a mixture of 1 part muriatic acid to 12 parts water.

To repair mortar joints in stone or masonry, first remove all loose or damaged mortar with a chisel and hand sledge. Remove no more mortar than necessary. Go easy with the sledge to avoid further damage. Use a metal bar or mortar hook to scrape out old mortar and create a clean surface. Flush with a hose. Mix a batch of firm mortar to pack the joints. Scrape away excess mortar so each joint is the same depth as the surrounding joints.

Wall Materials

1. BRICK
- Brick is a common material for walls.
- It is readily available and uniform in size.
- A wide range of patterns can be created with brick.
- Brick walls are long-lasting—limited only by the quality of construction and weathering of the mortar that holds it together.
- Brick is fairly costly.
- A tall wall takes skill to build properly.

2. CONCRETE
- Concrete is perhaps the most versatile material for walls.
- It can be poured into prefabricated forms.
- An effective use of concrete block is to build a plain wall, then face it with stone or brick.
- Concrete block can be covered with stucco—plaster that can be textured and stained before it is applied or painted after it dries.

3. STONE
- Stone is the most natural-looking material for a wall.
- Sometimes you can find the material in or near your garden.
- Stone adds permanence and structure without being imposing.
- With a little practice, it is easy to use.
- Stones of different sizes are necessary, because building a stone wall is like working a jigsaw puzzle.

4. COMBINATIONS
- Sometimes enough of one material is not affordable or available.
- Combining materials can result in a unique structure.
- A combination of materials can unify various elements of the garden.
- A combination wall can utilize materials you might not have considered, such as bottles or odd-shape pieces of metal.

Outdoor Living Areas
Terraces & Patios

Ideal for outdoor dining and entertaining, patios and terraces provide extra space to spread outside in good weather.

Expand your outdoor living options with a patio or terrace. What's the difference between the two? There are more similarities than differences; proximity to the house is the main distinction. Both usually are level areas with a firm surface that is paved. Generally, a terrace adjoins the house, whereas a patio may or may not be connected to the house.

No matter what you call them, these features—along with decks—are the workhorses of outdoor entertaining. For the sake of simplicity, both terraces and patios will be referred to as patios throughout this chapter.

Siting a patio

The success of a patio depends on its location. A patio's siting affects how much it is used and how well it serves the intended purpose.

If the patio is for outdoor dining, having it close to the house—and kitchen—increases the likelihood of its being used. A remotely located patio makes a great area for outdoor dining, but be realistic about how you respond to "out of sight, out of mind" situations. You may end up not using a remote patio as often as you had planned.

Another factor to consider when siting the patio is microclimate. A spot that is convenient to the kitchen may have too much or too little sun or an unpleasant view. Wind, sound, and privacy should also be considered. You may be able to screen unattractive views, add shade, or remove limbs to bring sunlight into the area. Or you may need to find another location for the patio. A master plan will help in dealing with these situations.

When planning a patio, consider the proximity of large trees that may suffer root damage or cause damage to the patio. Shallow roots can damage a patio over time. Also consider accessibility to electricity for lighting or water for a fountain.

Patio styles

The design of a patio should take into account the style of the house and the surrounding garden, as well as the purpose the patio is to serve. One of the first considerations is the size of the patio. Another consideration is levelness. A patio should provide a firm, level surface for seating and entertaining. That's one of the big advantages of a patio over a lawn, which can be a difficult base for setting up tables and chairs—especially after a rain, when it may be spongy or uneven.

Open and airy A patio is typically open, visually spilling into the surrounding areas. To avoid feeling exposed, consider adding a pergola or other overhead structure to give the patio a sense of containment.

Private and secluded A patio is a private outdoor room. You can create a sense of privacy by using the existing walls of the house or garage. You need not completely enclose the area as you would a courtyard. Instead, consider building a screen or fence to enclose part of the patio, leaving the other sides open. Partial enclosure creates a sense of intimacy, making the patio especially suited to outdoor dining.

Close to home Having a patio close to the house has many advantages. If it is visible from inside the house, it tends to be used more. A patio can also serve as a transitional area between the house and the garden.

Change of grade Add interest to a patio by having it slightly elevated or sunken. This is especially appropriate if your garden is relatively level. If you plan on setting the patio below the surrounding grade, you will need to add a catch basin that connects to an underground drain line. A raised patio will drain easily if you build the surface with a slight slope.

Underutilized area Sometimes paving a narrow side yard or other small area can turn an otherwise unused spot into a functional patio. This is especially true of areas that receive little sunlight and might be ill-suited to maintaining a lawn or other plantings.

opposite Several factors make a patio site successful. A wall, fence, or hedge creates privacy. The area should be large enough to include seating for meals and entertaining. Surround the area with attractive flowers, trees, and shrubs. Large containers bring greenery and color to deck locations.

Outdoor Living Areas:
Terraces & Patios

Patio Amenities

Furniture, lighting, and accents such as a fountain or plants contribute to a patio's overall look, usefulness, and enjoyment.

Furniture The most common and functional amenity for a patio is furniture. It provides a place to sit, dine, or otherwise enjoy the garden, and it helps organize the space. When choosing patio furniture, consider the style and how it coordinates with the surroundings, as well as how comfortable and durable it is. Outdoor furniture that has to be protected or stains easily when exposed to the elements will probably prove to be more trouble than it's worth. Invest in furniture that will stand up over time without a lot of extra care.

Lighting Add lighting to make the patio useful even after the sun goes down. If the patio is attached to the house, you can mount floodlights on the eaves for full illumination. Consider putting the lights on a rheostat so you can control the brightness. If the patio is not adjacent to the house, consider mounting lights on tree limbs, an arbor, wood posts, or decorative lampposts.

Covering A canopy over the patio provides shade and visually contains the area. Options include extending a lath or other open structure from the house (if the patio is adjacent to the house), building a freestanding structure, such as a pergola, or relying on the limbs of an existing shade tree. It is not necessary to provide a rainproof covering. It is more important to filter the sun and create the illusion of a roof. You might choose to have a canopy over part of the patio with the rest left open. This gives you another good option, because there are times when you want all the sun you can get on the patio.

Planting There are several ways to add plants to a patio setting. The easiest and most versatile is to use containers. Evergreen shrubs in containers can define areas of a patio, provide privacy and shade, or serve as a windbreak. Smaller pots of perennials, annuals, or bulbs can infuse seasonal color. One advantage to using containers is that they are portable, which means you can move the plants around to suit your mood and their needs.

top left Furnish patios with weather-resistant furnishings. All-weather wicker is durable and long-lasting. **above left** A change in level of just one step creates a sense of separation, even if the patio is close to the house. **left** A lattice wall planted with vines creates privacy on a small deck.

HOW TO ALLOCATE SPACE FOR OUTDOOR ENTERTAINING

1 ASSESS YOUR NEEDS.

Make a list of all the ways you want to use the patio. This list might include an area for reading and relaxing, or an intimate dinner for four, or a casual gathering of 20 friends. It may be all of the above and more.

As you enumerate the various uses for the patio, indicate which are most important to you. Many homeowners have an occasional need for the patio to accommodate large groups, but the vast majority of the time it needs to have enough room for only up to four people. One way to have a larger patio that still feels intimate is to frame part of the space with potted plants that can be moved when you need extra room.

2 DETERMINE THE TYPE AND AMOUNT OF FURNITURE REQUIRED.

Once you know how many people you need to accommodate, you can select furniture. Typically this includes tables, chairs, and benches. Note anything else you want in the space, such as a grill or drink cart.

If you already have or know the type of furniture you will use, measure all the pieces so you can plan the patio exactly. If you don't know what furniture you will have, you can use the general guidelines offered below.

3 CALCULATE THE AMOUNT OF SPACE YOU NEED.

The size of your patio is a personal decision, but there are some guidelines that may help you determine the right size for your needs.

If all you want is space for two people to sit with a small table in between, you can get by with a patio as small as 10 × 10 feet. Keep in mind that a patio this small may look out of place if it is next to the house.

For an adjacent patio, start with 10 × 20 feet as a minimum. That will provide enough room for four chairs and a small dining table.

As you map out the exact dimensions of the patio, plan for about 3 × 3 feet per chair to allow room for the chair and a comfort zone around it. The average garden bench requires about 6 × 3 feet.

Table sizes vary, but a standard bridge table is 3 × 3 feet. This may be too small for dining; the recommended space for a dining table for four people is 4 x 4 feet.

Sketch the general shape, size, and location of the patio onto grid paper, with each square equaling 6 inches. Then cut out pieces of paper to scale to represent chairs, tables, and benches. Move them around on the sketch to make sure you've allowed enough space. Be sure to leave room for people to walk around the furniture.

top When designing a patio, choose a style and materials that fit your personal taste and the surroundings. ***above*** Outdoor dining areas are more likely to be used when they are located close to the house.

Outdoor Living Areas: Terraces & Patios

Be sure that the containers match the style of the patio. For example, a whiskey barrel planter may look out of place on a formal brick patio where classic terra-cotta or dressy, painted wood planters such as Versailles tubs provide a more appropriate look.

Another alternative is to have built-in planting areas on the patio. Creating built-in beds is best done when you design and build the patio; leave open spaces to act as in-ground containers that you can plant in directly. In-ground planting creates more protection from freezing temperatures, and plants need less irrigation than if they are grown in containers. It also allows you to grow low groundcovers that help soften large expanses of paving.

If you include a built-in in-ground planter, it is vital that the planting hole drains adequately and soil does not become too alkaline as a result of adjoining mortar. For the best results, once the patio is built, excavate a hole at least 3 feet deep, do a percolation test, line the hole with heavy plastic, make several large slits in the bottom of the plastic so water can drain, then fill the hole with good soil.

Water features Whether elaborate and built-in or simple and freestanding, water features are desirable amenities for a patio.

Ornaments In the same way you would decorate a room inside the house, accent and otherwise decorate your patio with yard art. If the patio can be seen readily from inside the house, the use of ornament, such as wire spheres, metal obelisks, or topiary frames with or without plants, can help link the indoors with the outdoors.

Drainage Proper drainage is essential to a successful patio. This is especially true of a sunken terrace, which can quickly turn into a pond if it doesn't drain properly. A patio that is flush with or above ground can be drained by building it with a slight pitch that drains water off the patio and away from the house. It is important to plan the drainage before you build the patio.

left Consider the view from where you will be sitting. If it's attractive, you might frame it. *opposite above* A black-and-white theme pulls together two separate parts of a patio. *opposite left* Cutouts in the paving of a patio allow you to introduce trees and shrubs to the planting plan. *opposite middle* If your patio doesn't have a good view, create one with flowering shrubs and a simple structure such as this trellised arbor. *opposite right* The soothing sound of water on a patio can drown out unwanted noise.

Outdoor Living Areas
Decks

A standard feature of modern homes, decks bridge indoor and outdoor living.

Decks are as American as apple pie and have become a standard feature in landscapes from coast to coast. Yet decks have been used with frequency only since the 1950s, when home building boomed and rot-resistant lumber became readily available. Today, decks rival patios for the No. 1 spot for outdoor entertaining and relaxing.

Where to put a deck

When deciding where to put a deck, you don't have to settle for the obvious. Although a deck is ideal to create a level outdoor area on a sloping site, you can also build a deck on level ground. In most cases, decks can be built just about anywhere you would put a patio or terrace.

A deck can create an entry area. It can be a small, intimate space adjoining a bedroom or study. Or it can follow the typical model and be joined to the back of the house, with access from either the kitchen or family room. You can also build a freestanding deck in a remote area of the garden.

Your decision on where to build a deck should apply the same process of program development and site analysis as any major garden feature.

Uses for a deck

Most decks are attached to the rear of the house, which makes them true extensions of the home. Ideally, there is access from more than one room as well as the garden.

As an extension of the home, a deck takes its design cues from existing materials, colors, and overall style. Decks can be used for just about any purpose—entertaining, cooking, dining, gardening, or relaxing. Knowing how you intend to use the deck is helpful in designing the right structure.

If you plan to use the deck for large gatherings, estimate the number of people and include that information when designing the infrastructure. If you are building the deck yourself, check local building codes, regulations, and zoning restrictions. Height limits, overhead structures, construction parameters, and even where you can build this type of structure may be dictated by these rules.

Wood decks tend to have a softer, more casual effect on the landscape than terraces and patios built more formally of masonry such as bricks and mortar. They may also be much less costly to construct.

One of the strongest points about a deck is that it can make use of an otherwise difficult site. Building a deck over steeply sloping terrain is usually easier and less expensive than terracing the area. Because decks typically place you above the level of the surrounding land, they can command views of your property and beyond. The steeper the terrain, the higher the deck will be off the ground; planning calls for professional advice. Seek the counsel you need to be sure your structure is safe and enduring.

If you inherited a patio that is in poor shape, consider building a deck that sits just above the old concrete.

Combining a deck and patio

Decks seem to be an extension of the house, even those that are not literally attached to it. Patios seem more a part of the garden. This is partly due to their height. Decks are usually built just below the floor level of the house, whereas patios are built at ground level (or even below it).

Just as a patio that is adjacent to the house serves as a transition area between the house and garden, a deck plays the same role. Taking the idea of transition one step further, consider having a deck that is attached to the house step down to a patio. This creates a gradual movement from the completely controlled environment of the home to a wood-surface outdoor room next to the house to a stone-surface, ground-level room adjacent to or surrounded by the garden. If you are building a combination deck and patio, pay attention to where the two features meet. The union should be stable and safe, and the materials should match or blend.

Depending on how you plan to use your outdoor rooms, a combination deck and patio may provide one space used primarily as a sitting room and one dedicated to outdoor cooking and dining.

above Attention to detail makes a big difference, as with this bench and railing combination and the wood skirt that hides the deck framing. **right** With good design and quality construction, a deck can be an elegant addition to the home and landscape. Note the attention to detail where the steps blend with the patio. **far right** Add spots of brightness to a dining area with a red umbrella, matching seat cushions, and color coordinated plantings.

Stunning Structures
Arbors

An arbor is one of the most romantic structures in the garden. It can function as a focal point, an entryway, or a passageway.

An arbor is intimate in scale and limitless in style. There are many arbor kits on the market, but the average homeowner can easily custom-build one with basic tools and carpentry skills.

Before you start building, ask yourself: What do I want the arbor to accomplish? What style should I use? What materials? What finish? These questions will be answered in the following pages. As always, the best starting points for ideas on location, style, and use are your site analysis and master plan.

Using arbors

An arbor is versatile. Knowing how you will use it will help you decide where to place it as well as what style to choose.

Entry An arbor is ideal for marking an entry or indicating an opening along a fence line or hedge.

Using an arbor as an entry also creates a transition from one place to another—from the sidewalk to the garden, or from one part of the garden to another. Most people recognize arbors as passageways and are naturally drawn toward them. A subtle psychological effect occurs when one passes through an opening. You can enhance this experience by taking into account the views you would see as you pass through the arbor.

Double duty An arbor may draw the eye as a passageway does, but it is also a destination. The arbor can serve double duty if it is equipped with a bench or a swing.

Focal point Because an arbor frames a view with its basic shape, it makes a good focal point. The view can be part of the garden on the other side of the arbor, a distant view, or something within the arbor itself. An arbor placed against a solid fence or wall provides an ideal place to hang a frieze or plaque.

Arbor styles

The choice of style is based on personal preference and clues you get from the garden or your master plan. The key is to make the arbor part of a comprehensive plan. If the arbor is the first structure you will build, subsequent structures, such as fences and deck railings, should mirror the details used on the arbor.

opposite An arbor offers a leg up for flowering vines such as roses, clematis, and trumpet vine.

If you paint the arbor white or a bright color, it will attract attention, so it should be able to hold up to scrutiny and fit in with the rest of the garden. If you plan to cover the arbor with climbing plants—especially evergreens—style is less important, because the arbor will be hidden. A review of common arbor styles may be useful.

Formal Most arbors fit into this category. They are ornate and often painted white. They have a permanent, ordered sense about them that projects an attitude throughout the garden. Such arbors evoke images of formal estates, in America and England. This is worth noting, because the garden styles that gave rise to the prominence of arbors may or may not be appropriate for your garden.

If you like the look of an arbor but are unsure whether it fits your garden, choose a formal style and finish it with a dark stain or paint that plays down its prominence but still has impact when you are up close.

Informal An informal arbor is more playful and evokes a sense of fun instead of order. Because it can be made from a wide range of materials, colors, and fanciful styles, this type of arbor is more versatile. With styles ranging from contemporary chic to Medieval romantic, you can match the arbor to almost any style of architecture or garden, although it may look out of place in a formal garden or against a formal fence or house.

You can make an informal arbor of almost any material. Unlike a formal design, the style and details of an informal arbor do not always need to be echoed in other structures. By virtue of its informality, you are communicating that there is a different type of order in your garden.

Rustic Usually made of tree limbs or split logs, this style of arbor is ideal as a transition from a wooded path to a casual garden. Any arbor lends itself as a support for growing vines, but a rustic arbor seems to beg for them. You may be hesitant to let vines cover a structure that cost you time and money. A rustic arbor gives the appearance of having been in place for a long time. If this style appeals to you, try to use materials you find on your property. Materials from off-site can detract from the impression of the arbor being part of the garden.

Stunning Structures: Arbors

Arbor materials

Just as the style of an arbor can set a mood in the garden, the same is true for the materials you use to build it. Although there are limitations to each material—primarily finished lumber, metal, and rough wood—it is up to you to mix and match materials and styles. For example, you could develop a traditional design but build the arbor out of old tree limbs.

Finished wood Most arbors are made of finished lumber. Wood is readily available, easy to work with, affordable, and comes in uniform sizes. Because most arbors are traditional or formal in design, the uniformity of the wood lends itself to this type of project. Finished lumber can also be treated to resist rotting, making it especially suitable for outdoor projects. It can be painted, stained, or allowed to weather naturally; each treatment results in a different effect. Finished lumber is also popular because most how-to instructions are based on this material—all you need are basic woodworking tools and skills.

Metal A beautiful material for an arbor, metal is the most enduring but the most costly. This is especially true if you want a custom-designed or custom-built arbor. However, there are many prefabricated metal arbors and arbor kits available in garden centers, home improvement stores, and mail-order catalogs that are more affordable.

Metal arbors have two distinct advantages over wood: They can withstand the pull of a woody vine, such as wisteria, and they are relatively impervious to the effects of moisture trapped by vines. To prevent rust, ensure the arbor has a triple coating of primer under a double coat of paint.

Rustic This style and its materials are not suited to every garden. Using uniform sizes of wood—whether bought or found—makes a rustic arbor easier to build. Even if you use naturally rot-resistant wood, such as cedar, expect the material to last only half as long as finished lumber. Join pieces with standard hardware. Using materials found on-site helps make the arbor look as if it belongs in your yard.

above left A dark stain enables an arbor to blend into the garden and allows bright flowers to take center stage. *left* This arbor is a destination that doesn't disappoint, treating the visitor to a shaded bench.

Arbor finishes

Adding a finish to a wood arbor benefits it significantly in two ways: It makes a big difference in the overall look of the arbor, and it prolongs the life of the structure.

Paint Most painted wood arbors are made of pressure-treated lumber. Always make certain the wood is dry before painting. Unless pressure-treated wood is labeled as cured, let the structure stand exposed to the sun and air for at least six weeks after building before you paint. Otherwise, the paint may bubble as the moisture in the wood tries to escape. Rot-resistant wood, such as cedar and redwood, usually comes cured or dried and often is not painted.

There are three methods for painting an arbor; each works equally well. Use a brush or sprayer to paint the structure when it is in place. Or paint part or all of the arbor while building it, and apply touch-up paint once it is in place.

Stain This finish is used most often on rot-resistant wood. Stain is much thinner than paint and tends to run more; most people find it easier to apply with a rag than a brush. Moisten the rag with stain and rub it on the wood. You can stain pressure-treated lumber—usually pine—to resemble cedar or redwood. You may prefer to use a clear sealer instead of a stain; a sealer prevents moisture from seeping into the wood while allowing the wood to weather to its natural color.

Vines Growing over and around an arbor, vines offer a finished look. When choosing a vine, you need to know how the plant attaches itself and what help, if any, you need to give it.

Unless you are planting an aggressive woody vine, such as wisteria, the plant won't threaten the structure. The thin strips of lattice found in many arbors are susceptible to rot, however, and vines trap moisture and prevent the sun and air from drying out the lattice.

Consider using annual vines too. They provide coverage during the growing season and allow the wood to dry in winter.

top right White is the most common color for finishing an arbor. It makes the structure stand out, even when covered with vines. ***above right*** If using a rot-resistant wood, such as cedar, you can allow it to age naturally. Left unsealed, this arbor will turn gray. ***right*** This open, formal metal arbor will eventually be covered with climbing roses. Metal is the best material for training vines because it won't rot.

Stunning Structures
Gazebos

These freestanding outdoor rooms offer a focal point for your landscape as well as a location for outdoor entertaining.

Gazebos are unique among garden structures. Whereas many other features enhance or become part of an outdoor room, a gazebo *is* an outdoor room. It has walls, a floor, and a ceiling. As such, its impact in the garden setting is, in most cases, rivaled only by that of the house itself. Building a gazebo from scratch is a fairly significant project in terms of time, expense, and expertise. Often a contractor is hired to build a gazebo, or a homeowner can build one from a kit.

It's important to select the right type of gazebo. For the greatest success, consider the intended use for the structure, the style, its location within the garden, the materials you will use to build it, and the details you will add. Details help a gazebo fulfill its purpose, and they add character so the gazebo is in keeping with the overall landscape.

The first step in planning the perfect gazebo is knowing how you intend to use it. There is no right or wrong way—it is a matter of personal choice. You may want the room to be a getaway or a retreat. It could include sleeping accommodations for warm, sultry nights. You may want a place to entertain, whether casually or formally. Or you may want to have a gazebo for its looks alone. Make a list of all the activities you want to do in the gazebo as well as other functions you want the gazebo to fulfill, including being a focal point. Let this list guide you through the decision-making process.

Gazebo styles

When choosing materials and a style for your gazebo, incorporate features and details from the architecture of the house or other existing and visible structures to tie the gazebo to the rest of the garden. A review of some common styles will help get you started.

Modern A contemporary gazebo stands out and makes a bold statement. This style is best suited to complement a contemporary house.

Traditional The traditional gazebo fits more garden styles, especially when you consider finishes. A natural stain on this structure allows it to blend into the landscape; the same structure painted white would stand out more.

Rustic A rustic gazebo could be made of rough-hewn logs and even be lashed together with rope. This style lends itself better than the others to a woodland setting.

Siting the gazebo

Deciding where to build your gazebo is strongly linked to how you plan to use it. Review your site analysis while going over the following suggestions.

Put it close to the house. If you plan to use the gazebo for entertaining—particularly dining—you might want it near the house. It will be more convenient in terms of cooking and serving, becoming an extension of the house. A gazebo is also ideal near structures such as a swimming pool or terrace. These areas are typically used a lot; having the shelter of the gazebo nearby enhances the experience of the existing structure and promotes the use of the gazebo.

Make it a destination. Instead of siting the gazebo where it's visible from the house, hide it. Make it a surprise you find when you round a corner of the garden path. Or tuck it away so discreetly that only those intimate with the garden will know it is there—ideal for creating a getaway or retreat. If you want it to be a retreat, site the gazebo as far from the parking area, play areas, or the street as possible. If you don't have such a place, consider creating a private nook.

Use it as a focal point. You might want a gazebo purely for its aesthetics. It can take on a sculptural quality that makes it the dominant part of the garden. Keep scale in mind. If you have a small garden, design a small gazebo—a large one, no matter how attractive, would look out of place.

You can also use a part of the gazebo as the focal point, such as the roof peeking out from above a hedge, to draw visitors into the garden and help create a sense of intrigue.

If you want the gazebo to serve as a focal point, consider all the views from which you want to see it. In most cases there is more than one vantage point.

opposite A gazebo at the edge of a property offers a visual as well as actual destination. A dining area and electric lighting make it an ideal after-dark entertaining area.

Stunning Structures: Gazebos

Consider the views. You need to consider what the views will be like once you are in the gazebo. Start by looking at your site analysis for particularly good views from your property. Note any views you want to avoid. Keep in mind that the walls and ceiling of the structure can be used to frame views. If your gazebo will be a foot or two off the ground, stand on a footstool at the height of the finished level of the gazebo to check out the view. Alternatively, you could sink the floor of the gazebo a couple of feet if that's what it takes to achieve the best view.

Catch a breeze or a ray. Know the prevailing wind direction in the seasons you plan to use the gazebo. Orient the gazebo to take advantage of cooling breezes in summer or block chilly winds in early spring or fall. If you plan to have afternoon tea or morning coffee in the gazebo, site it to take advantage of the angle of the sun during those times. You may wish to orient the structure to frame the sunrise or sunset; site the gazebo so you will enjoy it.

Gazebo details

Details can make the experience of being in the gazebo more enjoyable. They can also make the gazebo look better and tie in to the rest of the garden.

Lighting This works in two ways. If the outside or inside of the gazebo is lit at night, the gazebo becomes a sculptural feature, drawing the eye from other parts of the garden and adding depth to the landscape. Lighting also extends the use of the gazebo by making it functional at night. When adding lighting to a gazebo, include a master switch from the house. In the gazebo, put the lights on a dimmer switch so you can adjust the lighting to match the mood as well as the ambient light. Before installing any lights that would illuminate the outside of the gazebo, stand in it at night to be sure the lights are not glaring in your face.

Cooling and heating A roof blocks the sun and makes the gazebo cooler, but it may also thwart breezes. A good way to keep the gazebo pleasant on even the hottest and muggiest days is to install a ceiling fan. If the design of the roof does not lend itself to a fan, or if it can't be adapted easily, consider using an oscillating fan. A fan also creates a pleasant white noise.

above left If you have an attractive view from your garden, a gazebo is a good way to get the most from it. *below left* Adding a gazebo close to a terrace or other structure is a good way to increase the use of both.

When it is comfortable enough to be outdoors with a light jacket or sweater, a source of heat will make your gazebo a cozy retreat. Tiki lamps, a built-in fireplace, or a fire pit just outside the gazebo can add charm and warmth. When siting a fire pit, be aware of prevailing winds; otherwise the smoke may run you out of the gazebo. Or consider an electric or kerosene space heater. Whenever you add heat to a wood structure, make certain you have a fire extinguisher on hand.

Seating Provide ample seating for the number of people you intend to have in the gazebo. The seating can be one continuous bench around the inside edge, or it can be a set of Adirondack chairs. Another possibility is a futon or a hammock for napping and overnight enjoyment.

Sound Adding sound blocks out unwanted noise and focuses attention inward. The sound can be soft music from a portable stereo or a built-in weatherproof one; the splashing of a nearby fountain; birds drawn to a nearby feeder and birdbath; the whir of a fan; or the crackle of a fire.

Utilities Wire the gazebo for basic utilities, even if you are unsure about how you will ultimately use the gazebo. Power is essential for a fan, lighting, a stereo, or a pump for a fountain. Consider having a nearby water source—especially helpful if you plan to use the gazebo for dining or if you need to douse the fire pit before calling it a night. Also consider a phone line, or an intercom if the gazebo is too far from the house for good reception from a home-based cordless phone. You can always turn off the ringer if you don't want to be interrupted.

above right A traditional gazebo, whether custom-made or built from a kit, offers an inviting respite from a sunny garden. ***right*** If you live in an area with biting insects, consider installing screens on your gazebo so you can enjoy it more often.

CHAPTER THREE

Creative Landscape Plantings

Enhance your yard with gorgeous easy-care permanent plantings: trees, shrubs, perennials, and roses.

above Lofty trees frame the front door of this quaint log home, while tidy shrubs shelter the foundation. Well-maintained woody plants add value to every home.
left Place blooming shrubs, such as this handsome dogwood, near your home where you'll regularly enjoy their beauty.

Trees & Shrubs
Woody Plants

Trees and shrubs are some of the most hardworking members of the landscape. They can change the whole look and feel of your yard.

Standing tall year-round, woody plants perform the essential functions of blocking chilly winter winds and casting valuable shade on exposed homes, lowering heating and cooling bills. While moderating temperatures in and around a home, trees and shrubs can also be employed to create a pretty living screen that blocks the views of a garage or neighboring property or prevents unwanted visitors from wandering into the yard.

These long-lived plants excel at many functional roles in the landscape; but don't let their task-oriented nature fool you. They do work hard, but they add beauty to the landscape at the same time. Plant a favorite magnolia or a flower-packed butterfly bush in your yard, and you'll instantly add easy-care color and texture.

Easy-care plants

Unlike annual flowers, trees and shrubs don't require planting every year. Woody plants thrive for at least 10 years to more than 100 years depending on the species. And unlike herbaceous perennials, many species of woody plants do not require frequent seasonal maintenance such as deadheading, pruning, or fertilizing.

Trees and shrubs do share some of the qualities of annuals and perennials, though: lovely flowers, intense fragrance, and intriguing foliage. Sweet-scented crabapples have pretty pink and white blooms that perfume the yard in early spring. Perfect for small landscapes, Japanese tree lilac bears frothy white blooms that add valuable color, texture, and fragrance in early summer. And long-lived oaks, maples, and many other trees fire up the fall skies with red, orange, and yellow foliage.

When combined with annuals and perennials, trees and shrubs create a multilayer landscape that ensures you'll be surrounded by beauty all 12 months of the year. When freezing temperatures zap the annuals and perennials, evergreen trees and shrubs will continue to provide color and form. A diverse landscape also supplies valuable food and shelter for wildlife year-round.

Long-term investment

Because woody plants are longtime members of the landscape, sometimes gracing a garden for multiple generations, it's important to thoughtfully consider how they will contribute to the look and feel of your space before planting. The next several pages detail many uses for trees and shrubs. You'll find a wealth of tips and ideas for plant selection and placement to make the very best use of trees and shrubs around your home.

MONEY TREE

Do trees, shrubs, and landscaping add value to your home? University studies indicate that they do indeed add value—a well-designed landscape that includes thriving, healthy plants increases your home value by as much as 12 percent.

The key to capitalizing on the value of landscaping is to landscape smart. Well-maintained trees and shrubs add far more to the bottom line than woody plants with broken limbs, crossing branches, and messy seedpods and fruit. Misplaced plants—those that are too close to a home or garage or those that encroach on walkways—are also detrimental. Easy-care plants will pay dividends and add charming curb appeal.

Trees & Shrubs
Creating Shade

Large leafy trees, such as oaks and maples, bring all-season beauty and cooling shade during summer.

A majestic oak or mighty maple is an intriguing landscape element for its sheer size. Look beyond the size of the long-lived tree, and you'll notice the curvaceous branching structure of oak provides valuable landscape interest year-round. And the maple likely lights up with hues of yellow, orange, and red in fall. Trees bring many aesthetic elements to your yard, and at the same time they cast valuable shade.

When thoughtfully placed, a tree can cast a shadow to cool a once sun-drenched patio. Or it can block sunlight from streaming in south-facing windows and raising the interior temperature of your home several degrees. Harness the power of shade that trees provide and you'll make your indoor and outdoor living spaces more inviting.

Deciduous trees—those that lose their leaves in fall—are the most common shade trees. Deciduous trees are especially useful for shading a dwelling because their foliage provides dense, light-blocking cover in summer when temperatures are high and the sun's warming effects are most potent. In winter the bare branches will allow sunlight to blanket a home, warming it a few degrees.

Get the most shade impact for your investment in trees by planting them on the southwest, west, or east side of a home. The sun is most intense from these directions, and well-placed trees will create shade most effectively.

Evergreen trees can also be employed as shade trees. They provide effective cooling in the summer, but because they retain their foliage year-round, they also prevent sun from filtering through in winter. Call on evergreens to shade the north or northwest side of a home, where winter sunlight is less of a factor.

Evergreens are also an excellent choice for outdoor rooms, which are rarely used in winter. The dense shade cast by Norway spruce or the graceful filtered shade of a white pine will create an inviting outdoor retreat.

A great shade tree

There isn't one particular species of tree that outranks others in creating shade. In fact, there are many great shade trees. Begin by considering the following qualities to determine what type of shade tree will complement your landscape.

Light shade or deep shade. A Norway maple casts dense, deep shade. The shade is so dense that grass has trouble growing under the canopy. This is a fine quality if the tree is near a patio or deck but can be frustrating if the tree is surrounded by lawn. A honey locust tree, on the other hand, creates dappled shade. A few rays of sunlight can easily filter through the fine foliage.

Easy care. Trees that are notoriously messy, dropping fruit or countless branches, make undesirable shade trees near a home. They'll quickly create more work than they are worth. Fall leaf drop is a given with deciduous trees. Autumn raking and minimal pruning should be all the care a mature shade tree requires.

Appropriate mature size. Trees are the longest-lived plants in a landscape. As they add years to their life, they add feet to their height and width. Too often people make the mistake of choosing a plant based on an inaccurate assumption about its mature size. A massive American sycamore grows up to 100 feet tall and nearly 40 feet spread at maturity. It's much too large for the average home landscape. Instead, aim for a tree that tops out at 40–60 feet tall and 30–40 feet spread.

opposite left Pair large trees with understory plants that thrive in low-light conditions to create a lush, easy-care landscape that will bring to mind a hike through the forest. **opposite, top right** 'Tricolor' beech is a large shade tree with lovely variegated foliage that turns yellow in fall. **opposite, middle right** This low-growing deciduous tree is just right for this one-story home. A lofty maple or oak would complement a two-story structure. **opposite, bottom right** Redbud, a small tree with charming heart-shape leaves, is perfect for small gardens and urban landscapes.

Trees & Shrubs
Planting for Privacy

You can build a fence to shield the view, but why not plant a living fence using trees and shrubs?

You can plant a well-maintained living fence that offers all-season color and texture, plus it provides a valuable habitat for wildlife.

While a typical fence is drab brown in spring, a Korean spice viburnum hedge, for example, is decorated with 2- to 3-inch-wide, clove-scent white flower clusters. Green fruit that turns red and then purple follows the flowers and is favored by birds. In fall, its green leaves turn burgundy and then intensify to dark purple. A wood fence is hard-pressed to compete with a viburnum's colorful show.

Deciduous trees and shrubs do an excellent job of creating privacy and muffling noise during the growing season, but their leafless branches provide little cover in winter. If year-round privacy is essential, choose an evergreen species. Evergreen rhododendrons and camellias offer beautiful blooms that rival those of popular deciduous shrubs while providing year-round privacy. Needled plants are always a good choice.

A living fence can mimic a traditional wood fence in style—a simple row of a single species of shrub, for example. Plants that tolerate pruning can be trimmed to create a formal appearance. For an informal privacy hedge, look to nature for inspiration. Plant a living screen using a mix of deciduous and evergreen species in a variety of heights and shapes. As the plants grow, maintain a consistent outer edge by pruning overly exuberant branches so the hedge does look overgrown.

left The flower-covered arching branches of Vanhoutte spirea are eye-catching for at least two weeks in spring. The pretty white flowers are delightfully fragrant.

Plant spacing will determine how quickly the hedge grows together. The closer together shrubs are planted, the faster their branches will meet to create a solid visual barrier. Situating plants too close together, though, can promote weak and spindly growth. A rule of thumb is to space plants no closer than half the distance of their mature width. For example, if the mature width of a shrub is 10 feet, space plants 5 feet apart for rapid coverage.

An ideal privacy planting

Many trees and shrubs create excellent visual barriers. When choosing plants for your living screen, keep these concepts in mind.

Evergreen versus deciduous. Evergreen trees and shrubs provide privacy 12 months a year. They are especially useful for shielding swimming areas and limiting views of a busy street or unsightly property. Evergreens also do an excellent job of creating a sound barrier.

Deciduous trees and shrubs often offer more varied flowers, foliage, and fragrance than their evergreen counterparts. Deciduous plants are excellent for shielding views in summer and fall, but they offer sparse coverage in winter and spring. Employ them in areas where year-round cover is not essential.

Appropriate size. Hedges vary in size from knee-high to lofty 20-foot-tall barriers. Some species naturally top out at 5–10 feet tall; these are much easier to maintain at 5 feet tall than a species that grows 20 feet tall. Width is another important factor. How wide do you envision your hedge? Be mindful of property lines.

Color and texture. Spring flowers, brilliant fall foliage, and clusters of bird-attracting berries all introduce color and texture into the landscape. Would you like a hedge that not only creates a barrier but also offers visual treats?

Ease of care. Some hedges require frequent pruning to maintain their good looks. Others take on a lovely, tidy appearance with little pruning. How much pruning are you willing to do?

SHADE-FRIENDLY TREES AND SHRUBS

Many trees and shrubs thrive in the shade. These shade lovers are called understory plants because they typically grow under the canopy of larger trees. Understory trees and shrubs thrive in filtered light and compete well with large trees for soil moisture and nutrients. Use these plants to create a living screen in a shaded landscape.

ARBORVITAE An evergreen shrub with soft foliage; will grow 20 feet tall but easy to maintain at lower height (pictured *above*).

BOXWOOD An evergreen with tiny glossy leaves; tolerates frequent shearing.

FOTHERGILLA A native deciduous shrub with fragrant spring flowers and brilliant color fall foliage.

SMOKE TREE An easy-to-grow shrub with purple-leaf cultivars and airy seed flowers in summer.

AMERICAN HOLLY An evergreen with bright red berries in winter; must plant male and female cultivars.

DOGWOOD A native tree with delightful spring flowers.

REDBUD A hardy plant whose vivid flowers cover leafless branches in early spring.

SERVICEBERRY A native tree with spring flowers, berries in summer, and colorful fall foliage (pictured *above*).

Screens & Windbreaks

A row of evergreen or deciduous trees or shrubs can help reroute the wind and save you money in winter heating costs.

A row of trees or shrubs, often called a windbreak, is a good match for whipping winter wind that sends your hat airborne the moment you step outside. When oriented perpendicular to the prevailing wind, a row of trees with dense foliage significantly reduces the wind speed. Evergreens serve this purpose well.

A windbreak, also called a shelterbelt, can reduce wind speed by as much as 50 percent. This is particularly helpful when the windbreak is situated near a house, where it will greatly slow wind and reduce heating-fuel consumption by as much as 25 percent.

The most effective windbreak consists of several rows of fast-growing, dense evergreen trees that reach a mature height of about one-and-a-half times the height of the house. Ideally the trees retain their stiff branches to ground level for maximum wind block.

Typically planted on the north and west sides of a home, a windbreak offers savings that increase as the portion of protected perimeter of a home increases. If a property doesn't have space for wind protection on multiple sides, add it where possible. Even a small windbreak will reduce heating costs.

Foundation plantings are also excellent at reducing wind speed and heat loss. Dense evergreen shrubs planted about 5 feet away from a house will create a trough of dead-air space. This dead-air space decreases heat loss from the house walls. Just like a traditional tree windbreak, a foundation-type windbreak is most effective on the north and west sides of a home, but the more foundation space covered, the greater the reduction in heat loss.

left A long row of columnar arborvitae is a living wall around this patio. The trees block wind and create privacy.

Useful and beautiful

A well-placed windbreak not only reduces winter heating costs, it also adds structure and form to the landscape. When choosing species for the windbreak planting, look for trees and shrubs that complement the style of your home and existing landscape elements. Here are a few more tips for creating a windbreak.

Location, location, location. The best windbreaks are planted in a line perpendicular to the prevailing winds. Windbreak plantings typically are installed on the north and west sides of a home. Wherever space permits, an extension of a windbreak will increase protection. Consider adding a row of trees to the east side of a home, too.

The distance the trees are planted from a home is important. The maximum zone of wind protection exists at five to seven times the height of the windbreak. For example, if the mature height of a windbreak is 50 feet, the trees should be planted 250–350 feet away from the home for maximum wind protection.

Mature size. A well-sited windbreak created using easy-care, long-lived trees can change from an asset to a headache if it outgrows its planting area and begins encroaching on your outdoor living space or the neighbor's property. Take time to consider the mature height and width of trees and shrubs when selecting species to create a windbreak.

Care requirements. The best windbreak plants require little annual care. Regular watering during the first growing season after planting and annual pruning when the plants are young is customary. A tree that has twig or branch drop requiring frequent cleanup is not a good choice. Choose plants that virtually take care of themselves. Limit maintenance around plants by blanketing the soil with a layer of organic mulch.

BEST WINDBREAK PLANTS

Count on these species to provide excellent wind protection. Choose small or dwarf varieties for wind protection near a foundation. Large plants make excellent windbreaks along property lines.

NORTHEAST AND MIDWEST
Arborvitae (pictured)
Eastern red cedar
Pine
Spruce
White fir

SOUTH AND SOUTHWEST
Crape myrtle
Eastern red cedar
Holly (pictured)
Loblolly pine
Southern magnolia

NORTHWEST
Bristlecone pine
Colorado blue spruce (pictured)
Eastern red cedar
Mugo pine
Rocky Mountain juniper

Trees & Shrubs

Year-Round Interest

Add color and texture to your landscape with a diverse selection of leafy, flowering, and evergreen trees and shrubs.

A landscape with year-round interest is ripe with color, texture, and beauty 365 days a year. A diverse palette of plants is essential to create a landscape that offers intrigue in spring, summer, fall, and winter. A thoughtful mix of trees and shrubs can easily ensure the view out a window in winter is just as lovely as the view in summer.

In most temperate climates, the growing season kicks off in spring, when many species of trees and shrubs unfurl colorful and often fragrant blossoms. Species bloom at different times throughout the spring and summer. Flowering quince, for example, is prized for its early bloom time. Its fragrant miniature-roselike flowers decorate leafless stems as soon as the soil begins to warm. Old-fashioned lilacs begin flowering later in the season. Stage a multiweek bloom show by pairing early-season blooming plants with those that bloom later. Foliage in shades of green, yellow, and purple adds color and texture to the garden in summer. A mix of leaf shapes will add energy to the landscape. Combine the simple oval leaves of magnolia with the petite foliage of European mountain ash. Another easy, energetic plant pair is a broadleaf plant with a needled plant—a maple with a white pine, for example.

The fall landscape lights up with shades of red, yellow, and orange and an occasional burst of purple or burgundy. A single magnificent tree displaying fall color can set an attractive seasonal scene. When choosing plants for fall color, don't overlook shrubs. Many shrubs have spectacular color on a small scale—an essential characteristic in small-space gardens.

Winter is a time of rest and renewal in the landscape, but shrubs with multicolor peeling bark, berries, or colorful twigs add a spark of energy to the quiet months in the garden. Gardeners in warm regions enjoy lovely camellia blossoms. Evergreen plants, such as pines, firs, and rhododendrons, are a pleasing contrast to the bare branches of deciduous trees.

Fuzzy buds, pretty peeling bark, and colorful twigs brighten the winter landscape. Include a few of these easy-to-grow beauties to decorate the yard in winter.

CRABAPPLE
Red, yellow, or green fruit persists into winter on some species of crabapple; small tree with spring flowers.

STAR MAGNOLIA
Conical buds are tightly closed through winter, but the velvety covering is eye-catching; large shrub or small tree.

PAPERBARK MAPLE
Bark peels and curls as the tree ages to reveal trunks mottled with shades of brown and red; small tree with colorful foliage.

REDTWIG DOGWOOD
Young twigs turn brilliant red in winter; promote vibrant twig color by cutting this shrub to ground level every spring.

HOLLY
Long-lasting red berries decorate plants for months in winter; must plant male and female plants for berry production.

Year-round good looks

A patioside planting, entryway border, or backyard hedge that offers beauty every day of the year is a valuable asset. Keep these tips in mind as you plan for year-round landscape beauty.

Plants that shine with interest in more than one season are always a good choice. Viburnums are an ideal example: Many varieties have striking spring blooms, and their leaves take on hues of red and purple in fall. Multiseason interest is essential in small landscapes where planting space is limited.

Offering color you can count on year-round, evergreen trees and shrubs are lovely backdrops for colorful deciduous plants in spring, summer, and fall. In winter, their dense oval and pyramidal forms reign supreme in the barren garden.

Get a jump on the spring bloom season by including trees and shrubs that wake up early. Witch hazel, camellia, daphne, and many viburnums begin blooming when there is still a smattering of snow on the ground.

Enjoy the antics of birds, butterflies, and other critters in the landscape by including plants that offer food and shelter.

opposite above Evergreen plants like the rhododendron and yew along this foundation offer color and texture year-round. **opposite below** Hydrangea flowers change color over the course of a growing season. These blossoms debut lime green, turn magenta, and fade to tawny brown. **top** Ring in spring with early-blooming trees and shrubs like this fragrant white crabapple. **above** Japanese maples are known for their intense fall color. Choose your favorite variety from hundreds of cultivars.

Trees & Shrubs
Wildlife Attractants

Offer food and shelter to birds, bees, and butterflies with a wide selection of trees and shrubs.

Put out the welcome mat for songbirds, squirrels, chipmunks, and a host of other backyard critters with trees and shrubs that offer them food and shelter. These easy-to-grow species are an especially welcome sight to creatures that are forced to travel farther and farther to find food in new subdivisions. Share the joy of landscaping for wildlife with your neighbors and create a neighborhood-wide habitat.

American Holly
Glossy evergreen leaves provide cover and nesting sites for a variety of wildlife. The large tree has fruit that draws songbirds, ruffed grouse, and deer.

Canadian Hemlock
Dense evergreen branches make this large tree an excellent shelter and nesting site. It also provides food for birds and small animals. It has graceful arching branches.

Oak
The acorns of these tall trees offer an important food source for both birds and mammals. Oaks also provide valuable nesting sites.

Rhododendron
Evergreen varieties of this shrub offer year-round cover. Spring flowers provide nectar for bees and butterflies. Rhododendrons thrive in shade.

left Evergreen trees like arborvitae offer shelter for many bird species, such as cardinals.

Crabapple

This small spring-blooming tree produces fruit relished by many songbirds and mammals. Butterflies and bees seek nectar from the plant's fragrant flowers.

Gray Dogwood

Fruit decorates this medium to large native shrub in fall, providing sustenance to birds during migration. It tolerates wet, dry, or poor soil.

Hackberry

An easy-to-grow, adaptable tree, hackberry produces fruit that attracts many bird species, including cedar waxwings, flickers, cardinals, and robins.

Hawthorn

These thorny trees are good nesting sites for birds. Hawthorns produce fruit eaten by cedar waxwings, sparrows, small mammals, and deer throughout winter.

Serviceberry

A small tree or large shrub, serviceberry produces fruit in early summer and attracts robins, cedar waxwings, rose-breasted grosbeaks, and other birds.

Staghorn Sumac

An ideal shrub for tough growing sites, staghorn sumac has fruit that persists through winter and is an important emergency food for a variety of birds in early spring.

Viburnum

Many varieties of these medium to large shrubs are attractive landscaping plants that provide fruit and cover for wildlife, particularly during late summer and fall migration.

Caraway

Caraway seeds can be used whole, such as sprinkled on breads and crackers, or ground and used in powder form.

Trees & Shrubs
Fabulous Fall Color

Glowing foliage ablaze with shades of orange, red, and yellow is a magnificent way to celebrate the changing seasons.

While many large trees light up with brilliant color in fall—maples, oaks, birches, and honey locust are just a few—hundreds of other woody plants also display color-rich leaves for several weeks in autumn. If planting space is limited, just one or two species prized for their autumn finery will easily create a lovely scene.

Color on a small scale
Shrubs and small ornamental trees offer a host of opportunities for adding color to petite suburban lots and courtyard gardens, where a massive oak isn't an option. The leaves of gray dogwood turn a velvety, rich deep red as the days get shorter. Oakleaf hydrangea sports Technicolor foliage in hues of red, orange, and yellow.

Shrubs and small ornamental trees are perfect for adding striking fall color to entryways, patioside plantings, and other popular outdoor areas calling for plants that maintain a small stature. Amplify the autumn coloring of deciduous plants by pairing them with evergreen shrubs. A dark green backdrop of yew or arborvitae is the perfect foil for a blazing-red crape myrtle.

Varying color
Decreasing day length and cooling temperatures trigger woody plants to prepare for winter. The plants' major visible preparation is changing leaf color. The process of leaf shedding, or senescence, is complex and closely connected to local ecology. Prior to leaves dropping from branches, plants absorb many sugars and amino acids from the leaves. These nutrients are used by the plant during winter, then fuel production of new leaves in spring.

opposite Temperature, moisture, day length, and soil conditions all influence how fall leaf color develops. Here, callery pear and sumac sport vibrant orange and red end-of-season color.

A RAINBOW OF COLORS
Add your favorite hues to the landscape with this roundup of colorful foliage. Some cultivars within a species produce more intense color than others. Be sure to read the plant tag to get a good idea of fall color potential.

YELLOW
Birch
Ginkgo (pictured top)
Honey locust
Hornbeam
Katsura tree

ORANGE
Staghorn sumac
Sugar maple

RED
Black gum
Burning bush
Callery pear
Red maple (pictured middle)
Japanese maple (pictured bottom)
Scarlet oak

PURPLE
Blackhaw viburnum
Smoke tree
Wayfaringtree viburnum

As sugars and amino acids are removed, other biochemical reactions break down components of the leaves, and the remaining components, which are responsible for fall coloration, become visible.

The hue and intensity of leaf color is influenced by growing conditions. A sweet gum tree might produce a bright red display one year and follow up with a dull red-brown cloak the following autumn. Soil moisture is a common factor in fall color production. Ample moisture often allows biochemical reactions inside leaf cells to be quick and efficient, then few of the colorful compounds are revealed. A dry growing season tends to produce the opposite effect.

Trees & Shrubs
Unique Bark & Twigs

Don't overlook the interesting aspects of some trees and shrubs.

Finely cut leaves, pretty berries, and fragrant flowers often overshadow the subtle, yet intriguing, bark and twigs of trees and shrubs during the growing season. As soon as fall turns to winter, peeling bark, zigzagging twigs, and a host of other lovely characteristics add style and glamour to the winter scene.

A leafless winter landscape calls attention to the lines and forms of trees and shrubs. Trees with pendulous branches, often called weeping, make a striking silhouette. The angular branching pattern of honey locust makes a bold statement against a pale blue winter sky. Leafless lilacs are a twiggy mass, while barren hydrangeas have a more open, upright habit.

When choosing trees and shrubs, take note of the lines and forms their leafless branches present in the landscape. In many regions, deciduous trees and shrubs are without leaves for at least six months a year—a surefire reason to consider their winter appearance.

Beauty of bark
The diverse character of bark is a surprise to many. Some trees and shrubs are cloaked with a smooth brown or gray protective coat; other plants have rough bark with many crevices. Play up the variation in texture by pairing opposing bark textures in a planting area.

Some of the most dramatic bark variations include unusual colors of bark. Many species of crape myrtle have warm cinnamon-color bark that brightens the winter landscape. Redtwig dogwood is beloved for its bright cherry-red twigs that are especially prominent against a snowy backdrop.

left Fast-growing gum tree has colorful, smooth bark. Thriving in warm regions, gum trees make good privacy screens.

Peeling, or exfoliating, bark adds another layer of interest to the landscape. A few popular trees with peeling bark include river birch, shagbark hickory, paperbark maple, and crape myrtle. Peeling bark tends to develop with age. A newly planted river birch, for example, will have little peeling bark, but by the time the trunk reaches 4–5 inches in diameter, it will be covered with curling paperlike strips of bark.

Some of the loveliest trees with peeling bark exhibit multiple hues when their outer layer of bark sloughs off. Lacebark pine does just that, revealing a patchwork of colors ranging from brown to gray to russet to green.

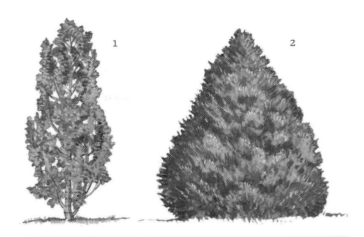

TREE AND SHRUB FORMS

Winter reveals the form of deciduous trees and shrubs. Knowledge of their forms is especially helpful when combining trees and shrubs in borders, such as foundation plantings, and in the overall landscape. For an energetic mix, pair plants with angular and rounded forms. For a calm, restful feel, combine similar plant forms. Here's a rundown of common forms.

Shrubs

1. COLUMNAR Like an arrow shooting toward the sky, a columnar shrub is a dramatic focal point.

2. PYRAMIDAL When seen from a distance, these shrubs tend to lift the eye upward. Plant them to contrast with a round or spreading tree.

3. SPREADING When paired with upright plants, spreading plants add interest at ground level while surpressing many weeds.

4. ROUNDED A perfect contrast to columnar plants, rounded shrubs are useful throughout the landscape.

Trees

5. ROUNDED OR OVAL Trees with this lovely shape often achieve their most perfect form when planted alone in an open yard. Or plant a group of three or five and enjoy their billowing mass.

6. PENDULOUS Ideal focal points, pendulous or weeping trees are lovely living sculptures.

7. SPREADING Useful for creating a canopy over a patio or continuing the horizontal line of a house, spreading trees will also frame a view.

8. VASE-SHAPE OR MULTISTEM Trees with vase shapes or multiple stems have a striking natural look. Plant several multistem trees together to achieve the look of a forest.

Perennials
Classic Combinations

Use color and flower form to create beautiful perennial pairings in your landscape and garden.

As you begin to plan perennial pairings, it's easy to focus on color. Another factor to consider is plant form. Juxtaposing forms enhances a garden's eye appeal. Get started with these proven combinations.

Round Flower + Wispy Form

Pair a rounded flower with a wispy plant form, such as combining wispy blue fescue and ball-like ornamental allium (plus later-blooming lilies).

Ornamental Allium + Blue Fescue

'Autumn Joy' Sedum + Russian Sage

Peony + 'Powis Castle' Artemisia

Coneflower + Pincushion Flower

Goldenrod + Allium

Airy Plant + Solid Plant

Place a plant with an airy, open form next to one with a more solid appearance. Many perennials qualify for this type of matchup. A perennial that seems open in form, such as a meadow rue, can appear more solid when paired with a dense ornamental grass, such as zebragrass.

Astilbe + Hosta

White Gaura + Showy Sedum

Yarrow + False Indigo

Fern + Heart-Leaf Bergenia

Spike Flower + Rounded Leaf

Towering blossom spikes look lovely when planted alongside perennials that unfurl rounded leaves. The counterpoint of slender and curving forms creates eye-catching beauty and adds up to design success.

Ligularia + Hosta

Delphinium + Lady's Mantle

Cardinal Flower + Coralbells

Gayfeather + Showy Sedum

Perennials

Grasses

Beautiful and textural grasses add so much to a landscape. Use them with perennial flowers or other grasses.

Ornamental grasses introduce elements of movement and rhythm to a perennial garden. With colorful foliage that lingers through winter, grasses also provide year-round interest.

Blue Oatgrass
Steel blue foliage; wheat-color seed heads. 24 inches tall and wide; seed heads to 40–64 inches tall. Zones 3–9.

'Bowles Golden' Sedge
Golden yellow leaves turn green as they mature. 24–36 inches tall and wide. Zones 5–9.

'Positano' Miscanthus
Green leaves with silver midrib; seed heads reddish. 5–6 feet tall; seed heads to 7 feet. 3–5 feet wide. Zones 5–9.

'Rigoletto' Miscanthus
White-striped leaves; seed heads red fading to silver. 3–4 feet tall; seed heads to 5 feet tall. 30–36 inches wide. Zones 5–9.

left Grasses offer a kinetic energy to the landscape as well as look lovely all winter, even encrusted in snow.

Feather Reedgrass
In winter, green leaves turn tan; purple-green seed heads turn gold. 3–4 feet tall; seed heads 5 to more than 6 feet tall. 2–3 feet wide. Zones 4–9.

Golden Hakonegrass
Gold leaves striped dark green. 18 inches tall and wide. Zones 4–9.

'Morning Light' Miscanthus
Green leaves striped with creamy-white edges; pinkish seed heads fade to silver. 5 feet tall; seed heads to 6 feet. 3 feet wide. Zones 6–9.

Muhlygrass
Green leaves; purple-pink to pink-red seed heads fade to gold in fall. 12 inches tall; seed heads to 36 inches. 3–4 feet wide. Zones 6–10.

Porcupinegrass
Horizontal yellow bands on green leaves; pinkish seed heads. 5 feet tall; seed heads to 7 feet. 3–4 feet wide. Zones 5–9.

Switchgrass 'Prairie Fire'
Blue-green foliage turns red in summer; seed heads rosy red. 36 inches tall; seed heads to 4 feet. 24 inches wide. Zones 4–9.

Perennials
Texture

Combine plants with coarse, medium, and fine leaves to create a tapestry of texture in your landscape.

In the garden, texture consists of several components. Visual appearance as related to touch—what a plant feels like—is one aspect. The blossoms of bearded iris resemble richly hued velvet with fuzzy epaulets. Oriental poppies look like crepe-paper blooms atop pipe-cleaner stems. Astilbe and meadowsweet unfurl flowers resembling feathery plumes, and foamflower and meadow rue showcase lacy blooms.

Leaves also introduce touchable content to the perennial palette. For instance, lamb's-ears looks and feels soft and woolly. Yellow corydalis bears divided leaves perfect for tickling, many ferns resemble feathers, and some hostas unfurl seersucker foliage. Golden hakonegrass resembles a soft waterfall, and the spiny foliage of globe thistle threatens danger. Each introduces texture to a perennial garden.

How a plant absorbs or reflects light is another aspect of texture. Light absorption enhances a leaf's textural appearance. The shiny leaves of bugleweed and Lenten rose stand out in a planting more than the matte foliage of campanula and hyssop.

Leaf or flower size also contributes to texture. Large leaves bear a bolder presence than small ones. For example, coralbells or hosta leaves present a stronger texture than fine ornamental grass foliage or a fern's divided leaves. A black-eyed Susan flower has a stronger presence than airy foamy bells blooms.

Textural categories
Typically leaves and flowers are classified as coarse, medium, or fine in texture. A coarse-texture plant has large leaves and flowers, large teeth along leaf edges, or rough surfaces. Fine-texture plants have small or narrow leaves and flowers or finely divided leaves. Medium-texture plants fall between coarse and fine and can take on either a coarse or fine appearance, depending on what's growing nearby.

left Intentionally mingling foliage textures gives a garden that magic factor that makes you pause to take in the beauty. Glowing golden hakonegrass plays a fine-leaf textural counterpoint to a broadleaf hosta.

Texture isn't a characteristic cast in stone; it's truly relative. While coreopsis and muhlygrass always appear fine-texture, goldenrod can look fine-texture next to a broadleaf hosta but coarse-texture next to an airy ornamental grass.

Some plants don different textures at various points in the season. Lady's mantle flowers present a fine texture; its leaves, medium. Pincushion flower foliage is medium-texture, but when flowers appear and dance atop wiry stems, the plant assumes a fine-texture look.

Design with texture

Use texture to your advantage when assembling a perennial bed. While combining flower colors is necessary, focus on foliage as well. Blossoms last a short time, but leaves linger. By carefully composing textural compositions, the garden border will strike interesting chords all season long. Use contrasting textures to introduce lively refrains and groupings of similar textures to play a soothing tune.

In shade gardens, texture saves the day when flowers fade and all that remains is green foliage. If you're facing a shady site, stage a textural drama punctuated with colorful foliage.

Play with texture to manipulate perspective in the garden. Fine-texture plants placed at the back of a garden give a sense of infinite expanse. Coarse-texture beauties planted at the rear of a large bed shrink a space, bringing the far end closer. Gardens viewed from afar benefit from a selection of coarse-texture perennials, which are easier to see.

TOPS IN TEXTURE

Perennials fall into three general categories of texture: fine, medium, and coarse. Mix plants from each category to create striking combinations. Medium-texture perennials can frequently function as fine- or coarse-texture, depending on their planting partners.

FINE-TEXTURE
Astilbe Part shade to full shade (pictured)
Boltonia Full sun to part shade
Lavender Full sun
Prairie dropseed grass Full sun
Silvermound artemisia Full sun

MEDIUM-TEXTURE
Butterfly weed Full sun
False indigo Full sun to part sun (pictured)
Hyssop Full sun to part shade
Ladybells Full sun to part shade
Siberian iris Full sun to part shade

COARSE-TEXTURE
Bear's breeches Full sun to part shade in cool regions; full shade in hot regions
Heart-leaf brunnera Part shade (pictured)
Hollyhock Full sun
Hosta Part to full shade
Rodgersia Part sun to full shade

Perennials

Single-Hue Gardens

Perennials bloom in a wide range of colors. Creating a design using just one color can add unity to your landscape.

For a simple but sophisticated approach to perennial garden design, create a monochromatic planting. In this type of design, you use plants that unfurl leaves or flowers in a single color and in hues, shades, tints, and tones of that color. The result is a foolproof design featuring colors that don't clash or create too much contrast.

If your passion is red, a monochromatic garden celebrating that color could include expressions of red, such as burgundy, scarlet, orange-red, carmine, cerise, and pink. For a purple garden, you could work in plants featuring lavender, blue-violet, violet, lilac, periwinkle, mauve, and eggplant. No matter what hue you choose to be the centerpiece of your garden design, you'll want to include a few touches of a complementary or analogous color throughout the planting to stir interest.

Single-color strategy

A monochromatic scheme provides an opportunity to use color to open up a small or shade-shrouded garden. By planting perennials in pastel pink, blue, or yellow, you can make a small space feel larger or turn up the light in a shady corner. Avoid using pastel hues in sunny spots if you'll view the area during the day, because the sun will wash out the colors, making them appear white. At dusk, however, these pale colors reflect light, forming a glowing welcome for after-dinner garden walks.

Count on gray to add neutral filler to the garden, forming a buffer zone that underscores subtle shifts between various expressions of the featured color. Group plants of a single color

above left In a monochromatic planting, include foliage plants and annual bloomers that suit the scheme. Here, burgundy-splashed 'Iron Cross' oxalis, bee balm, and annual impatiens add red tones to the garden all season long. **below left** In a blue garden, consider adding blue-tone pinks, such as chives, to the mix. Use white as a foil that graciously interrupts the monochromatic scheme.

family just as you would different-color plants. Create contrast by placing a dark shade next to a lighter tint and by blending foliage textures.

Remember to work colorful foliage into your design. You can find perennials and shrubs that bear leaves in a broad range of hues, including yellow, purple, burgundy, and blue. Use these foliage stars to accent and complete your monochromatic scheme.

Sculpture, furniture, or garden decor can also support your color choice—or introduce a contrasting accent. Look for hardscape that complements your color scheme, such as stepping-stones, tiles, or pavers. Mulch can play a supporting role in the design, blending in or interjecting a quietly subdued contrast. It's wise to surround a monochromatic garden with a swath of lawn or a single-color path to provide a place for the eye to rest and serve as a foreground or backdrop to the monochromatic bed.

Shift your focus

Following a monochromatic approach transforms the design process into an exercise in considering aspects of plants beyond flower and foliage color. Form and texture—of both leaves and plants—play stronger roles in the perennial-selection process when color is removed from the equation.

If you rely on flowers to carry the garden through the seasons, ensure that something is always blooming. An easy way to do that is to visit a full-service garden center every three weeks throughout the growing season to see what's in flower and to give you ideas on perennials to include in your garden.

As with any perennial garden, a monochromatic planting is a work in progress. Make changes over time as you spot weaknesses in the color scheme or downtimes in the flower show. Interject daubs of complementary color if the overall effect shifts from monochromatic to monotonous at any point during the growing season.

GARDEN BLUES

Blue is one of the more elusive colors in the garden. While there are shades and tints of blue varying from purple to pale lavender, true blues are hard to find. Satisfy your appetite for blue with a few of these blue-tone beauties.

1. BALLOON FLOWER Blue-violet balloon buds burst open to reveal star-shape flowers from early summer to fall. Zones 4–9.
2. CLUSTERED BELLFLOWER Clustered violet bell-shape blooms top stems in early summer. Zones 3–8.
3. CARYOPTERIS Fluffy blue flower clusters fill stems from late summer to early fall. Zones 4–8.
4. BLUE FESCUE Compact grass with tufts of blue foliage. Zones 4–8.
5. 'BLUE PANDA' CORYDALIS Blue fishlike flowers dangle over fine foliage from mid-spring to early summer and repeat bloom in fall. Zones 5–9.
6. MONKSHOOD Blue blossoms cover spikes from late summer into fall. Zones 3–8.
7. GLOBE THISTLE Blue flower spheres stand on gray-green stems in midsummer and linger for weeks. Zones 3–10.
8. 'HALCYON' HOSTA Steel-blue leaves unfurl from spring through frost; reportedly shows some slug resistance. Zones 3–8.
9. NEW ENGLAND ASTER Daisylike flowers cover mounding plants from late summer into fall. Zones 4–8.
10. 'MAY NIGHT' SALVIA Deep blue flower spikes stand above foliage in late spring and linger for weeks. Zones 4–10.

Perennials
Foliage

White, silver, gray, and black leaves can infuse perennial combinations with a quiet beauty.

Set aside the color wheel, and you'll discover several other colors that deserve a place in your garden. These hardworking hues earn top billing and solve problems in garden design. White, silver, gray, and black can infuse perennial combinations with that mystical wow factor.

White, silver, and gray

Because white reflects light, it's a showstopper in the garden, grabbing attention in a way that's second only to yellow. Pure white deserves particular consideration in conditions where light is lacking—a shady nook, a moonlit garden, or a woodland setting. Another excellent place to lean on white is in a planting bed backed with dark evergreens. Count on white to enliven spring and fall settings, when sunlight is not as harsh as during high summer.

Pair white with green to cast an elegant ambience; mix it with pink, lavender, and other pastels for a demure, restful setting. Call on white to referee a clash between bold colors. Take care not to sprinkle white haphazardly throughout a planting. Too much can stir chaos, pitting bold perennials against one another in a bid for attention.

Silver and gray put the finishing touches on a perennial bed, their mellow personalities coaxing other colors into harmony. Throughout the perennial garden, position silver and gray plants to soothe clashing colors, emphasize a deep-tone plant, or highlight a focal-point plant. In low-light situations, silver and gray reflect light, adopting a luminous quality. You can also rely on silver and gray plants to spark interest when nearby bloomers are not in flower.

left Dark-leaf perennials, such as 'Hillside Black Beauty' bugbane, introduce deep shades to the garden that form exquisite pairings with light-tone flowers or chartreuse foliage.

Black in the garden

Most plants sold or labeled as black are actually a deep, deep purple or burgundy. From a distance, these shades appear black. You can find "black" hollyhocks, irises, butterfly bushes, tulips, and roses—all featuring flowers in the deepest shades. Dark-foliage plants, such as 'Black Jack' sedum, black mondograss, 'Black Adder' mountain flax, 'Hillside Black Beauty' bugbane, and 'Obsidian' coralbells, also impress.

Dark colors in a garden pair naturally with pastel hues. A pale pink catmint with a deep purple bearded iris forms a sizzling partnership that fills late spring and early summer with riveting beauty. Back a dark-flowered butterfly bush with Japanese silvergrass for a sparkling summer scene. Dark foliage also delivers an eye-pleasing jolt when partnered with gold. Pair 'Black Beauty' or 'Obsidian' coralbells with 'Bowles Golden' sedge, or 'Black Jack' sedum with porcupinegrass, and you'll have season-long drama.

Site dark plants—whether the deep hue resides in flowers or foliage—in sunny areas of the garden. Tucked into shade, these bass-tone beauties tend to disappear.

Green, gold, and other hues

Leaves unfurl in many shades, tones, and tints of green. Take time to study the variations on a green theme at a garden center. Remember that the greenery in your garden will play background music through most of the garden season. When perennials aren't flowering—whether it's a momentary rest or a prolonged pause—greens take up the melody. Choose perennials with an eye toward a mix of green.

Foliage also offers other colors: gold, white, burgundy, blue, purple, rose, silver, and variegated. Incorporate striking leafy stars into your perennial design. Don't overdo variegated foliage; site it carefully for the biggest impact. Gold-leaf foliage plants tend to grow the strongest color in sunny sites, although a hot, dry footing can produce leaf scorch. White-leaf plants typically thrive in light shade.

A SILVER LINING

Add a silver sheen to your perennial beds with plants that unfurl leaves in silver or gray shades. While most of these plants open blossoms at some point in the growing season, their foliage introduces a steady shot of color all season long. Rely on these perennials to stage a vibrant contrast with bold-color beauties or infuse a garden with a soft glow at dusk.

SILVER-FOLIAGE STANDOUTS

Artemisia	'Silver Shimmers' lungwort
'Jack Frost' brunnera	Mullein
'Pewter Veil' coralbells	Rose campion
Japanese painted fern	Russian sage
Lamb's-ears	Silver sage
Lavender	Silver speedwell
Lavender cotton	'Moonshine' yarrow

PERENNIALS: BLOOM COLORS

Use this chart like a color wheel. From left to right, the colors go from warm to cool.

THE WARM RANGE

'Paprika' yarrow

Oriental poppy

Yellow-and-white bearded iris

'Fire and Ice' hosta

Red Asiatic lily

'Enchantment' lily

Yellow chrysanthemum

'Sea Foam' foamflower

'Anzac' daylily

'Golden Grace' chrysanthemum

Lily

Golden hakonegrass

'Ideal Crimson' pinks

Orange Asiatic lily

'Sarah' chrysanthemum

'American Sweetheart' hosta

Autumn sage

'Nicole' chrysanthemum

Evening primrose

'Golden Tiara' hosta

Red-orange daylily

Black-eyed Susan

Daylily

Green hosta

'Fires of Fuji' daylily

Yellow torch lily

Cushion spurge

Barrenwort

Crocosmia

Yellow corydalis

Lady's mantle

'Don Stevens' hosta

THE COOL RANGE

'Krossa Regal' hosta

Globe thistle

Caryopteris

Bloody cranesbill

Lamb's-ears

Balloon flower

'Johnson's Blue' geranium

New England aster

Blue oatgrass

Delphinium

'Blackberry Wine' corydalis

Spiderwort

'Elvis Lives' hosta

'Black and Blue' blue anise sage

Jackman clematis

Stoke's aster

'Blue Panda' corydalis

Columbine hybrid

'May Night' salvia

'Berry Exciting' corydalis

'Butterfly Blue' delphinium

'Iso-No-Nami' Japanese iris

Bearded iris hybrid

Centranthus

'Georgia Blue' creeping Veronica

Siberian iris

Columbine hybrid

'Niobe' clematis

Heart-leaf brunnera

Clustered bellflower

Rose verbena

Lenten rose hybrid

PERENNIALS: BLOOM TIMES

With plants listed alphabetically by common name, this chart shows the bloom period of many popular perennials (E=early, M=midseason, L=late). It also displays peak times for other decorative features, such as exceptional foliage, winter structure, or ornamental seed heads. Dark green bars show typical bloom times; light green bars represent visual interest. Consult this chart to make beds and borders look good from spring to fall.

	BLOOM TIME
	VISUAL INTEREST

PLANT NAME	SPRING			SUMMER			FALL			WINTER		
	E	M	L	E	M	L	E	M	L	E	M	L
Allegheny foamflower		bloom						visual				
Anise hyssop					bloom							
Artemisia				visual	visual	visual						
Asiatic hybrid lily				bloom								
Aster						bloom	bloom					
Astilbe				bloom								
'Autumn Joy' sedum					bloom	bloom						
			visual	visual	visual	visual	visual	visual				
Baby's breath				bloom								
Balloon flower				bloom								

PLANT NAME	SPRING			SUMMER			FALL			WINTER		
	E	M	L	E	M	L	E	M	L	E	M	L
Bear's foot hellebore	bloom											bloom
	visual	visual	visual	visual	visual	visual	visual	visual	visual	visual	visual	visual
Bee balm					bloom							
Bethlehem sage	bloom	bloom										
			visual	visual	visual	visual	visual	visual	visual			
Big blue lobelia						bloom						
Bigleaf ligularia					bloom							
			visual	visual	visual							
Bigroot geranium			bloom	bloom								
			visual	visual	visual	visual	visual	visual				
Black-eyed Susan					bloom	bloom						
						visual	visual					
Blanket flower					bloom	bloom						
Blue oatgrass			visual	visual	visual	visual	visual	visual	visual	visual	visual	visual

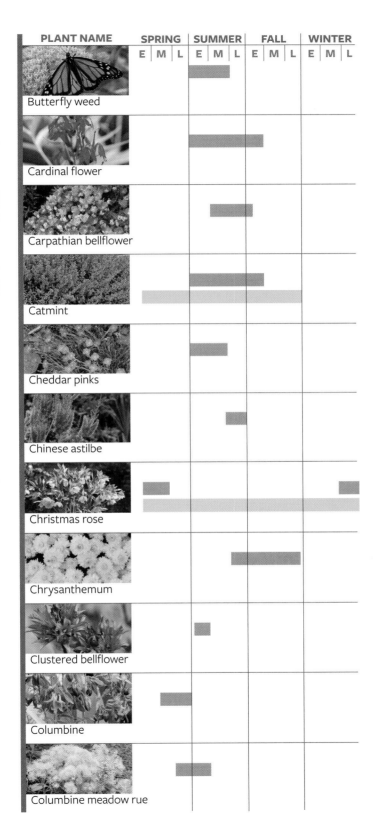

PLANT NAME	Spring E	Spring M	Spring L	Summer E	Summer M	Summer L	Fall E	Fall M	Fall L	Winter E	Winter M	Winter L
Butterfly weed				■	■							
Cardinal flower					■	■						
Carpathian bellflower					■							
Catmint			▫	■	■	▫	▫					
Cheddar pinks				■	■							
Chinese astilbe						■						
Christmas rose	■	▫	▫	▫	▫	▫	▫	▫	▫	▫	▫	■
Chrysanthemum							■	■				
Clustered bellflower				■								
Columbine			■									
Columbine meadow rue				■								

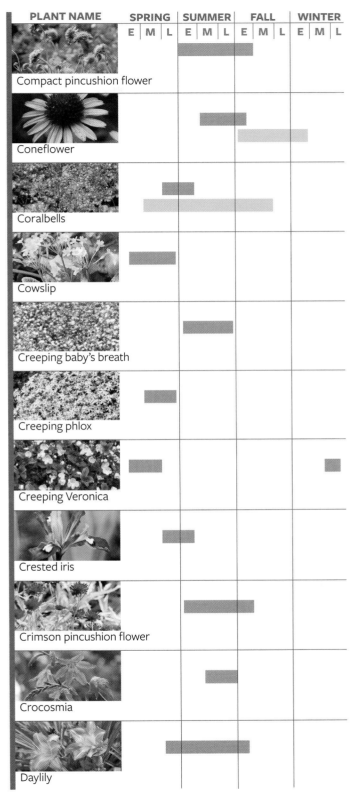

PLANT NAME	Spring E	Spring M	Spring L	Summer E	Summer M	Summer L	Fall E	Fall M	Fall L	Winter E	Winter M	Winter L
Compact pincushion flower				■	■							
Coneflower					■	■	▫	▫				
Coralbells			■	▫	▫	▫	▫					
Cowslip		■	■									
Creeping baby's breath					■							
Creeping phlox		■										
Creeping Veronica			■									■
Crested iris			■									
Crimson pincushion flower				■	■							
Crocosmia					■							
Daylily				■	■							

PLANT NAME	SPRING			SUMMER			FALL			WINTER		
	E	M	L	E	M	L	E	M	L	E	M	L
Evening primrose, sundrops				▪								
False indigo			▪									
False Solomon's seal	▪	▪										
Feather reedgrass				▪	▪							
						▪	▪	▪				
Fernleaf yarrow				▪	▪							
		▪	▪	▪	▪							
Fleabane			▪	▪								
Foamy bells			▪	▪								
		▪	▪	▪	▪	▪	▪					
Fragrant bugbane							▪					
Frikart's aster					▪							
Garden phlox					▪							
Gayfeather				▪			▪					

PLANT NAME	SPRING			SUMMER			FALL			WINTER		
	E	M	L	E	M	L	E	M	L	E	M	L
Globe thistle					▪							
Gloriosa daisy					▪	▪						
Goatsbeard				▪								
Goldenrod						▪	▪					
Ground clematis					▪							
Hardy begonia							▪					
Hardy hibiscus							▪					
Heart-leaf bergenia	▪											
		▪	▪	▪	▪	▪	▪	▪	▪	▪	▪	▪
Heart-leaf brunnera	▪	▪										
		▪	▪	▪	▪	▪	▪					
Helenium							▪					
Hollyhock				▪								

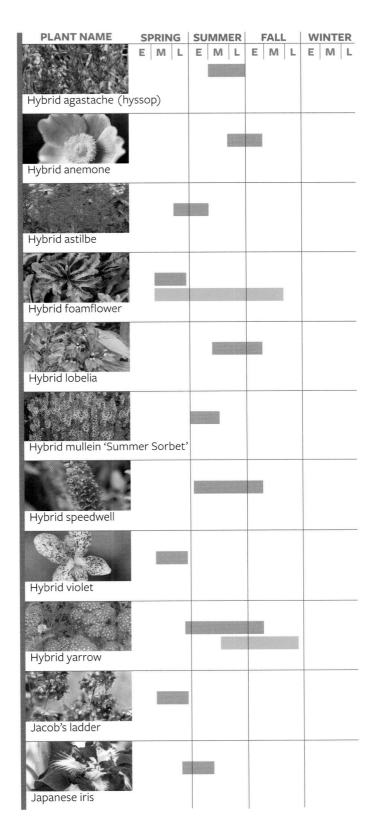

PLANT NAME	SPRING E	M	L	SUMMER E	M	L	FALL E	M	L	WINTER E	M	L
Hybrid agastache (hyssop)				●	●							
Hybrid anemone					●	●						
Hybrid astilbe			●									
Hybrid foamflower		●	●									
Hybrid lobelia					●	●						
Hybrid mullein 'Summer Sorbet'			●									
Hybrid speedwell				●	●	●						
Hybrid violet		●										
Hybrid yarrow				●	●	●						
Jacob's ladder		●										
Japanese iris			●									

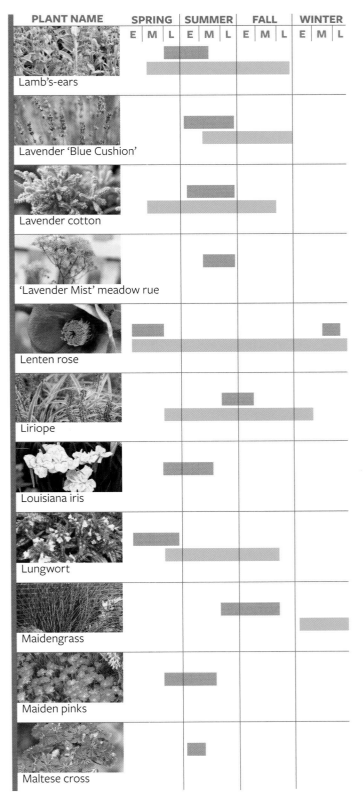

PLANT NAME	SPRING E	M	L	SUMMER E	M	L	FALL E	M	L	WINTER E	M	L
Lamb's-ears		●	●									
Lavender 'Blue Cushion'				●	●							
Lavender cotton				●	●							
'Lavender Mist' meadow rue												
Lenten rose	●											●
Liriope						●	●					
Louisiana iris				●								
Lungwort	●	●										
Maidengrass							●	●				●
Maiden pinks				●								
Maltese cross					●							

Perennial bloom times continued.

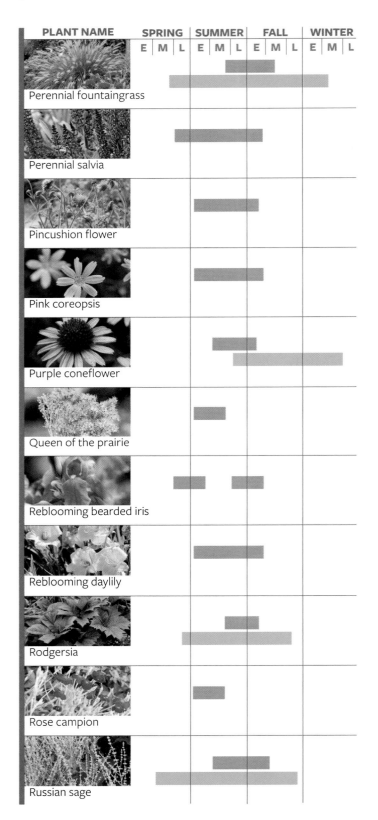

PLANT NAME	SPRING E	M	L	SUMMER E	M	L	FALL E	M	L	WINTER E	M	L
Moss phlox	■	■	■									
Moss phlox	■	■	■	■	■	■	■					
Nettle-leaved mullein				■	■							
Obedient plant						■	■					
Old-fashioned bleeding heart			■									
Olympic mullein				■								
Oriental hybrid lily						■						
Oriental poppy			■	■								
Ornamental onion				■	■							
Ornamental onion					■	■						
Ornamental oregano					■							
Ozark sundrops				■	■	■						
Pacific bleeding heart		■	■				■	■				

PLANT NAME	SPRING E	M	L	SUMMER E	M	L	FALL E	M	L	WINTER E	M	L
Perennial fountaingrass							■	■				
Perennial fountaingrass				■	■	■	■	■	■	■		
Perennial salvia				■	■	■						
Pincushion flower					■							
Pink coreopsis					■							
Purple coneflower						■	■					
Purple coneflower							■	■	■	■		
Queen of the prairie				■								
Reblooming bearded iris				■			■					
Reblooming daylily					■	■						
Rodgersia							■					
Rodgersia						■	■					
Rose campion				■								
Russian sage							■	■				
Russian sage				■	■	■	■	■	■			

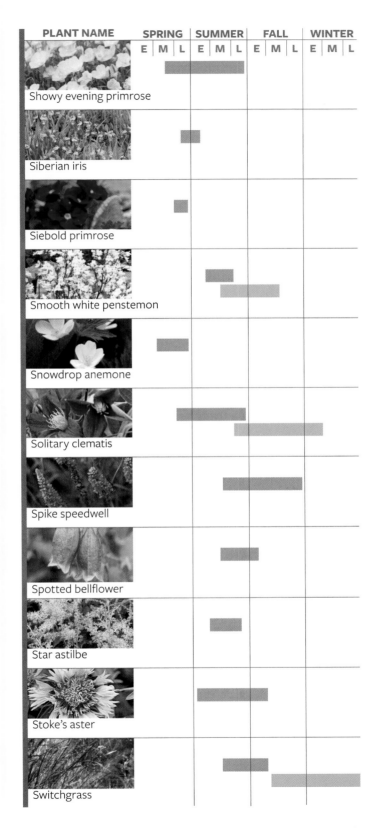

PLANT NAME	Spring E	Spring M	Spring L	Summer E	Summer M	Summer L	Fall E	Fall M	Fall L	Winter E	Winter M	Winter L
Showy evening primrose			■	■	■							
Siberian iris				■								
Siebold primrose			■									
Smooth white penstemon				■	■							
(Smooth white penstemon, lower)				■	■	■						
Snowdrop anemone		■										
Solitary clematis			■	■	■							
(Solitary clematis, lower)					■	■	■					
Spike speedwell					■	■						
Spotted bellflower				■								
Star astilbe				■								
Stoke's aster				■	■							
Switchgrass					■	■						
(Switchgrass, lower)							■	■				

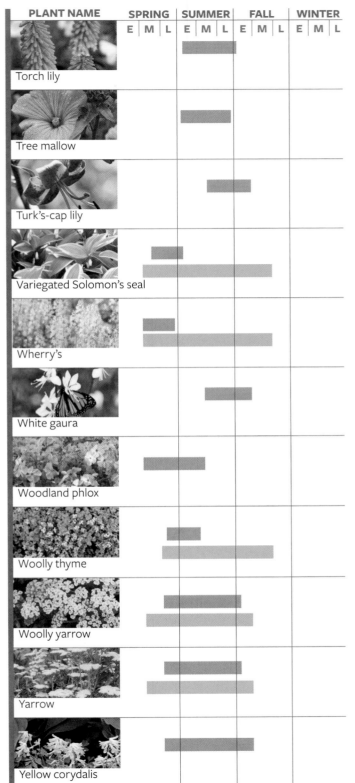

PLANT NAME	Spring E	Spring M	Spring L	Summer E	Summer M	Summer L	Fall E	Fall M	Fall L	Winter E	Winter M	Winter L
Torch lily				■	■							
Tree mallow				■								
Turk's-cap lily					■							
Variegated Solomon's seal			■	■								
(Variegated Solomon's seal, lower)			■	■	■	■	■					
Wherry's			■	■								
(Wherry's, lower)			■	■	■	■	■					
White gaura					■							
Woodland phlox			■									
Woolly thyme				■								
(Woolly thyme, lower)				■	■							
Woolly yarrow				■	■							
(Woolly yarrow, lower)				■	■	■						
Yarrow				■	■							
(Yarrow, lower)				■	■	■						
Yellow corydalis				■	■	■						

Roses

Solving Slopes

In addition to being beautiful, roses can show their hardworking side when utilized as groundcovers in hard-to-plant areas.

A slope, even a moderately steep one, need not be a problem planting area. If attractively terraced, it can be an ideal location for almost any kind of rose. A slope provides ready-made drainage, and walls or embankments are perfect places to fill with improved soil.

Some yards have spots you'd want to cover with attractive plantings—and then basically ignore. With a little planning, you can use roses to fulfill this purpose admirably.

Groundcover roses

Most roses touted as groundcovers do not truly fit that definition. Some are simply low-growing shrubs, others are very upright, and some grow with a slight spreading habit. To allow them to cover the ground, they must be planted very closely together—1 foot apart or less. Most of the Flower Carpet varieties fall into this category.

Low-growing rugosas are even more suitable as groundcovers. If grown on their own roots, rugosas have a tendency to sucker and spread into unfilled areas, eventually presenting a mass of color on a low-maintenance plant.

A few rose varieties grow long, low, relatively lax canes that can truly be considered groundcovers. These include 'Sea Foam', with white blooms on canes that can reach 6 feet or more, and 'Red Ribbons', with lax canes between 4 and 6 feet. The next best: 'Max Graf', a once-blooming rugosa hybrid with single pink blooms, and 'Nozomi', a miniature with 3- to 4-foot-long lax canes. Many of the ramblers can also be used effectively as groundcovers.

Making more plants

To cover a large area, gardeners can propagate plants using a process known as layering, similar to creating new strawberry plants from runners.

About 3 feet or farther from the mother plant, pin one of the long canes to the ground with a piece of strong wire, such as coat hanger wire, being careful not to cut into the bark. Cover the pinned spot with a little soil. Within a few months, new roots will form where the cane meets the soil. Once the new plant gets established, remove the pin and cut the cane between the new growth and the mother plant.

Caring for groundcover roses

Although many groundcover roses are touted as care-free, they produce more flowers when spent blooms are removed (deadheading). This is especially true for low-growing rugosas. Avoid thinking of them as plants that can thrive without attention. They grow best with fertilizer once or twice in the spring and summer, plus they need watering even after they are established. Many are winter hardy to Zones 4 or 5 with little to no winter protection.

opposite left Use the many heights and sizes of roses to create layers of color within sloped and terraced beds. *opposite, top right* Groundcover roses stabilize and beautify a sunny hillside. *opposite, above right* 'Red Ribbons', a highly rated shrub rose, grows with canes long enough to flop over and cover the ground. *opposite right* Raised beds offer good drainage and the opportunity to amend and improve the soil.

Roses

Mass Plantings

Roses are one of the most beautiful ways to achieve floral color in the landscape.

What's more beautiful than a running line of blooming roses alongside a fence or property line?

Nothing catches the eye of a garden visitor like a mass planting of one rose variety. That bright wall of color makes a focal point like no other. Mass plantings can include tight groupings of three plants, a linear hedge, or a border of dozens of plants. Generally, the more plants used, the greater the visual impact.

For best effect, choose a rose variety that grows no taller than about 4 feet. The best selections for mass plantings include heavy-blooming floribundas, polyanthas, and shrubs. Walls, other structures, or evergreens serve as effective backdrops to set off the brilliant colors.

Close neighbors require care

When designing a mass planting, check the plant tag to see how wide the rose bush grows. Roses in a mass display should be planted about 1 foot apart for the best blooming display. However, planting roses close together makes it more difficult to care for them.

left Plant tough shrub roses next to a see-through fence, such as split rail or ornamental iron, for an extra-decorative effect. **opposite above** Use color as a mass-planting opportunity. The yellow 'Behold' miniature rose shields the leggy lower portions of the 'St. Patrick' hybrid tea. **opposite below** Spaced close together, 'Martha's Vineyard' shrub roses make an effective and beautiful hedge.

Use these guidelines when massing roses:

Plant no more than two bushes wide when making a border or a hedge, so plants can be approached from either side.

Keep tight circles of bushes no larger than 3 feet wide to allow access to all plants from the outside. A larger arrangement creates a hard-to-reach area inside.

Choose disease-resistant varieties for mass plantings, because problems will spread more quickly than among wider-spaced plants.

Roses as hedges

An old adage claims that fences make good neighbors. Using roses to create a hedge or fill a border is a most beautiful fulfillment of this promise. A rose hedge can play the role of a living fence, serve as a visual privacy hedge, or simply create a garden room. If you want privacy, however, remember that roses drop their leaves for winter in most areas of the country.

Decide how tall you want your hedge to be, choose an attractive variety, then determine its spreading habit to decide how closely to plant the bushes. The closer they are planted to one another, the more quickly a hedge will fill out.

Varieties touted as hedge roses often are not the best choice for this purpose. Shrubs work well, as do hybrid rugosas, which can reach up to 6 feet tall. Rugosas can be pruned lower, if needed, require no spraying and little water, and display attractive hips and varying foliage colors in autumn. Most shrubs and all rugosas are generally hardy in most areas of the country.

CHAPTER FOUR

Maintaining Your Landscape

Keep your garden and landscape in tip-top shape in every season with easy-care tips and techniques.

Prepping Your Planting Beds

Planting a beautiful bed or border is easy when you follow some simple gardening techniques.

Clearing vegetation

Clear existing vegetation from garden sites using one of several methods. The process you choose depends on how much time you have, how much effort you want to invest, and the kind of vegetation you're removing.

If you're dealing with turf or a groundcover, physical removal will work effectively. For a planting bed laced with pernicious weeds, such as quackgrass, dandelions, mugwort, or wiregrass, you'll need an aggressive stance to eradicate them.

Whichever method you use, define the bed edge before beginning. Use a sharp spade to slice into vegetation. With the blade inserted into the soil, rock the spade back and forth to form an accessible trench. If you use an herbicide to remove vegetation, create a physical barrier or shield using cardboard, plastic, or lumber to prevent any spray from drifting onto surrounding plants.

Method 1: Physically remove vegetation

Removing plants by hand involves intensive labor but offers a low-cost approach to clearing a bed. When digging vegetation by hand, budget roughly an hour to hand-clear 100 square feet, although that estimate varies based on the type of vegetation

left Use a supple garden hose to define a bed outline. View the bed from interior rooms and outdoor living areas. When you're satisfied with the shape, outline the edge with flour and start digging.

you're removing. Sod comes up easily, as do some groundcovers. If you face deep-rooted perennial weeds, you'll have to dig deeper, which will slow your progress.

When clearing vegetation by hand, remove as little soil as possible; the top few inches of soil is the most fertile. As you start removing the first chunks of existing vegetation, examine the soil beneath. You shouldn't see any grass rhizomes, plant roots, or rooted stems. If you do, dig a little deeper and remove more soil.

When working with a groundcover that roots along stems, search around in the proposed garden site and locate crowns of the plant. Focus on digging those out; the remaining stems should pull up easily.

Method 2: Use an herbicide

An herbicide eradicates weeds and turf in short order, killing the aboveground portion of plants, roots, or both. It's an excellent choice when time is short. Read the package label; typically you can plant in an herbicide-treated area within 14 days. One of the most commonly used herbicides for killing grass and weeds is glyphosate.

If you aspire to an organic garden, you might not want to use herbicides. Many professionals in the prairie-restoration movement, which generally embraces organic principles, use an herbicide such as glyphosate, which becomes inactive in soil after a few days, to prepare planting areas and wipe out existing nonnative plants.

An excellent use for herbicides is on a slope. Spray plant tops with herbicide, and roots will remain to hold soil in place. When greenery dies down, you can dig through the remaining roots to plant perennials. Within two years, you won't see any sign of the previous vegetation.

If you need to wipe out weedy roots, spray plants in late fall, when carbohydrates are moving from leaves into roots. At this time, herbicides move more readily into roots, and you should be free of problem weeds come spring.

SOD STORIES

When you remove turf, you're left with a pile of sod. Recycle those pieces using these ideas.

Patch and repair bare spots in your lawn.

Add pieces to the compost pile. Toss turf onto the pile upside down, so the grass will decompose and not root into your compost pile.

Share with others. If you can't use your sod, ask neighbors or gardening friends if they would like it.

TURF'S UP

Learn the basics about how to remove existing turf in a potential planting site.

TO REMOVE TURF, begin with a sharpened spade blade. Starting along your defined edge, push the spade under the grass. Use short pushes to slice about 1 inch under turf. You might start the process standing up, but you'll need to kneel before you finish.

A MANUAL SOD CUTTER requires muscles and elbow grease to operate. Its main benefit over removing turf with a spade is that it keeps you off your hands and knees. It's not any easier in terms of physical labor. Use this method for a small garden area.

RENT A MECHANICAL SOD CUTTER if you're clearing a large garden space. This method lifts sod easily and in strips that form ready-to-use patches for bare spots in your lawn. A mechanical sod cutter can shave hours of labor from clearing a garden site.

CHOOSE AN HERBICIDE for weed-infested turf or when you're short on time. Use a sprayer that delivers large droplets. Don't spray on a windy day or you risk damaging nearby plantings. The herbicide must coat foliage to kill the plant, so don't mow or trim leaves before spraying.

Planting: Prepping Your Planting Beds

Slower methods to clear vegetation

Slower methods to clear vegetation get beds ready in four weeks to a year.

Method 1: Smothering

Smothering works by depriving plants of sunlight. Typically, a smothered bed is ready for planting in six to 12 months. Spread layers of material over existing plants, starting with a layer—cardboard, 10 layered sheets of newspaper, or dark plastic—that allows no sunlight to penetrate. Use mulch, such as compost, grass clippings, straw, or chopped leaves, for the second layer. Many gardeners start a layered bed in fall; the bed is ready in spring.

"Lasagna gardening" works well when you know you'll be constructing a new bed in a certain place. Start with a light, impervious layer and add layers as they're available. At any point during the process, if the layers are deep enough or the soil beneath is diggable, you can bury kitchen waste in the same area to attract and feed beneficial soil organisms.

Method 2: Solarization

Solarization is an excellent choice for a heavily weed-infested site. With solarization, you harness the sun's energy to bake the soil above 140°F to kill weed seeds, insect eggs, disease spores, and nematodes. Cut down weeds and till up roots with a heavy-duty tiller. Rake weeds and stems, and rake a second time to even out the soil. Water the area thoroughly to soak the top 4–6 inches of soil. Cover the soil with a sheet of clear construction-grade plastic (1–6 mil), stretching it tightly. Seal any seams with clear tape to trap heat generated beneath the plastic. Use heavy blocks or bricks to hold down the edges until you can bury them to anchor the plastic and retain heat. In four to six weeks, the soil will be sufficiently heated and you can plant.

Amendments

When you have removed existing vegetation, it's time to work amendments into the soil. This task is the most labor-intensive aspect of planting a perennial garden. The goal in working the soil is to improve drainage on lower levels, if needed, and to work organic matter into the upper 6–8 inches of soil.

left In the Northern Hemisphere, the best time to solarize the soil is when the sun is at its highest point in the sky: June and July. This method works best in a garden site that receives at least six hours of direct sun daily.

As you blend in amendments, try to create gradual changes in the soil from top to bottom. Work in amendments from the top down, aiming to increase organic matter in the topmost layer, where the majority of soil organisms and plant feeder roots are. Lower soil layers might need only to be broken up to enhance drainage. Before digging, make sure soil isn't overly wet or dry.

Mix in amendments by hand, using a digging fork or round-point spade. Hand-digging makes sense in a small garden or to save money. Going over the ground two or three times with a spade will effectively blend amendments into the soil. For a large garden, rent or borrow a rototiller. A tiller isn't effective in rocky soil or a bed filled with tree roots, but it works fast in sandy or loamy soil. In clay soils, don't churn the same area of soil too much which could compact lower layers where digging tines strike.

In soil with many tree roots, a digging fork (also called a spading fork) maneuvers well without damaging roots. A digging fork also makes quick work of soil preparation in sandy soil.

To mix in amendments, add a 1- to 2-inch layer of organic matter on top of the soil and work it into the top 6–8 inches. If digging by hand, use a digging fork to turn forkfuls of soil on its side, mixing in the amendments as you turn the soil. Repeat, adding another 1 inch of organic matter plus any other amendments. Dig these amendments in 3–4 inches deep. This amending method yields a gradual decrease in organic matter from the soil surface to deeper layers.

JUST-RIGHT SOIL

Avoid working soil that's overly wet or dry— you might make the soil structure worse, not better. This is most important for soil with clay particles; sandy or high-silt soils aren't an issue. Before digging, grab a handful of soil and squeeze it.

JUST-RIGHT SOIL: CLUMPS IN HAND When soil is right for digging, it forms a ball that breaks apart easily when touched. No water drips from it as you squeeze.

TOO-DRY SOIL: DUSTY Soil that's too dry to work won't clump together. Too-dry soil creates a dust cloud if you dig in it, and topsoil blows away. If you work too-dry soil, a hard crust forms on the surface when water touches it.

TOO-WET SOIL: MUDDY When you squeeze a clump of soil that's too wet, you end up with a wet, muddy hand. Too-wet soil sticks to digging tools and, if you dig in it, forms hard clods that clump together.

TOUGH WEEDS

When you deal with tough weeds, such as the taproots of dandelions or spreading quackgrass, don't give up. Try one of these methods to bid weeds good-bye.

Spray and till. Use an herbicide to kill pernicious weeds. When the weeds are dead, rake them out by tilling the soil. Tilling brings weed seeds to the surface, so wait a few weeks for those seeds to sprout, then spray again. A third till-and-wait period will ensure a weed-free garden.

Solarize. Solarization kills even the most persistent weed seeds and roots, and the soil is ready to plant in four to six weeks.

Smother. If time is not an issue, smothering persistent weeds over winter will kill them.

Planting Successfully

The hardest part of planning a landscape is definitely the preparation work.

Planting even a large border takes a small fraction of time compared with clearing vegetation and blending amendments into soil. Before planting, transfer your garden design from paper to the planting bed. For each plant (tree, shrub, and perennial), you'll need to know the mature size. If your plants are in pots with plant tags, look for that information on the tag. For perennial starts obtained from neighbors or friends, research mature size.

Arrange your plants in the garden, starting at one point and working outward. Place the plants slowly and carefully, situating them with the correct spacing for their mature size. You might want to let potted trees, shrubs, and perennials sit in the landscape plan for a few days to view the design from several angles (inside and out) and confirm that you're satisfied with it.

Best time to plant

Aim to plant at a time of year when the plants are able to sink roots with the least amount of stress. In cold climates, planting in late spring or early summer provides perennials an entire season to grow before winter cold arrives. Early spring and fall are ideal times to add trees and shrubs to your landscape. Fall is an ideal planting time in mild regions, where winter brings moist soil and cool air without freezing temperatures. For climates with clearly defined wet and dry seasons, plant perennials at the start of the rainy season and allow rainfall to irrigate the plants.

left Before planting, arrange perennials on the soil according to your garden design. Stand back and inspect the placement, then begin tucking plants into soil.

Mulch

Newly landscaped beds need a layer of mulch to maintain soil moisture and suppress weeds. Adding mulch after planting works well when you're dealing with trees and shrubs, and large perennials—quart or gallon size. For small and bare-root perennials, it's often easier to mulch the bed before planting. To plant, simply pull back mulch and dig a planting hole.

Mulch quality and type vary immensely. You don't have to pay top dollar to get the best mulch product; you can find inexpensive sources of quality mulch. Many communities gather and compost yard waste and offer it to gardeners at little or no cost.

Before taking advantage of what appears to be the best mulch bargain in town, discover how the mulch is processed. If compost is not turned but just sits and decomposes, you might take home compost laced with weed seeds and disease spores. In that case, the bargain is a problem in the making.

Often you can find well-composted manure free for the taking at stables or farms. In coastal areas where there's a fish-based industry, many companies offer free fish-waste compost.

Mulch sold in bulk is cheaper than bagged products. Look for discounted bagged mulch during end-of-season sales at seasonal garden centers, the kind sold at grocery and warehouse stores during the growing season.

When you use organic mulch, such as bark, pine straw, shredded leaves, or compost, you can usually identify potential problems by scent. If you detect an odor of ammonia, vinegar, sulfur, or alcohol, that mulch could burn plants. In general, if you can't stand the mulch smell for about 10 seconds, you don't want that mulch. Mulch that's safe to place around plants has a damp, earthy odor.

MULCH HOW-TO
Learn proper mulching techniques with these simple steps.

1 MULCH TO PROPER DEPTH

Apply a 2- to 4-inch layer. Thicker layers can lead to rodent or pest problems. If mulch breaks down quickly in your region, it's better to apply two thin layers over the course of a year than to apply one thick layer.

2 MULCH AWAY FROM CROWN

Pull mulch about 2–4 inches away from perennial crowns. Mounding mulch over crowns can lead to rot and provide a safe haven for voles and other plant-munching critters.

3 WATER AFTER APPLYING

Water dry mulch after applying it to help hold a dry, light material in place, rather than letting the wind blow it away.

BHG TEST GARDEN TIP

PERENNIAL PLANTING DEPTH

Most perennials flourish when their crowns are planted at the same depth as in the growing container. Test planting depth by laying a tool handle across the planting hole with the perennial placed at the proposed planting depth in the hole. Adjust the soil in the planting hole accordingly. When the crown is even with the tool handle, the plant is at the proper depth. Exceptions to the ground-level planting rule include these:

Above-grade. Perennials prone to rot grow better when their crowns are slightly above soil level. These include daylily, lady's mantle, lamb's-ears, and bearded iris.

Shallow depth. Perennials that crave moisture thrive when their crowns are 1–2 inches below grade. Examples, as well as how deep to plant, are bee balm (1 inch), bugbane (2 inches), hosta (1 inch), and peony (1 inch deep in warm climates, 2–3 inches deep in cold zones).

Planting: Planting Successfully

Digging the perfect hole

Tucking plants into beds requires some attention to detail, but mostly it's an easy, approachable task. Dig a hole that's no deeper than the height of the root ball and a few inches wider than the container. Remove any rocks you unearth while digging. With a bare-root perennial, form a mound in the base of the planting hole to hold the crown and allow roots to spread out and down.

The right tool

Tackle planting with a variety of digging tools. Specialized tools suited to specific tasks make quick work of planting, but you can manage your garden with a few key implements. A **digging spade or round-point spade** creates a sharp, straight bed edging. It's also useful for digging holes for large plants. A **short-handle shovel,** sometimes sold as a contractor's shovel, works well for digging small holes. The short handle is easy to manage while on your knees, which makes it handy for planting.

A **transplanting spade** has a long, narrow blade that fits neatly between established perennials. It's the digging tool of choice when you're working in an existing planting bed, maneuvering and digging around plants. For small perennials in 2- or 4-inch pots, a **hand trowel or hoe** speeds up planting, especially when soil is loose and easy to dig.

Pots, roots, and crowns

When dealing with container perennials, water plants thoroughly before planting. To remove plants from pots, invert the container with one hand splayed over the soil and cradling the stems. If the plant doesn't slide out easily, lay the container on the ground and roll it, pressing down with your hands using some force. You can also step on the pot, but use light pressure to avoid damaging the plant.

After removing the plant from the pot, if roots blanket the outside of the soil, tease some free or slice about ½ inch into the root ball at several points. The idea is to loosen and free roots to branch into surrounding soil after planting. If you don't loosen roots, they'll tend to circle inside the planting hole, which will stunt top growth.

POSTPLANTING CARE

After planting, place mulch around perennials, covering any exposed soil. If you mulched before planting, replace mulch around plants. Water thoroughly, soaking the top 8 inches of soil. Dig into soil away from plants to determine saturation depth. Watering settles soil and removes air pockets. If water starts to run off before soil is adequately soaked, stop for 30–45 minutes before resuming irrigation.

New perennials need evenly moist soil to root and establish. Typically 1 inch of water per week, delivered through rainfall or watering, is sufficient. Pull back mulch and check soil moisture 3–4 inches deep to determine whether you need to water. Established perennial gardens need about ½ inch of water per week. Moisture-craving plants need more; drought-tolerant plants need less.

Before planting, brush soil away from around the base of the stems so you can see the crown. This will help you place the plant at the correct planting depth.

Remove a biodegradable pot before planting as long as roots aren't poking through the pot and the pot isn't decaying. A dry, intact biodegradable pot can restrain roots after planting, preventing them from invading surrounding soil.

left After setting a perennial into soil, begin to backfill the planting hole, tamping soil into the empty spaces. When the soil is even with the surrounding bed, add mulch.

Planting
Edging Your Beds

Garden edging makes a bed look neat and complete. Plus, it makes mowing around the bed easier.

Garden edging dresses beds with the outdoor equivalent of a string of pearls. A neat bed edge gives a garden a polished, professional finish—but it delivers much more than good looks. Edging also serves a purpose, establishing an effective border control over the potential turf war between perennials and surrounding grass.

Look at edging as another aspect of structure in your garden, a material that can provide year-round interest. Select from a variety of manufactured edgings, or create your own using natural or recycled materials. Stones, shells, or large-diameter broken branches provide effective, organic edging. Natural materials decompose over time, which makes them an excellent choice when your garden is a work in progress and you haven't yet discovered the perfect edging.

A twist on the classic Southern bottle tree is bottle edging, which features upside-down glass bottles inserted into the soil around beds. Colored glass evokes the most charm. Push bottles into the soil to varying depths to create an undulating effect. Recycle past-its-prime garden gear into an edging, such as terra-cotta pots placed upside down along beds or tool heads with broken handles shoved into the soil.

left Edging can be purely functional, or it can combine beauty with function. Mortared stone dresses a bed with pleasing curves.
opposite A deep-trench edge treatment gives planting beds a neat appearance that's easy to maintain. A quick pass with a string trimmer along bed edges keeps the look sharp and clean.

Evaluate your options

Approach edging from a budget-minded stance by starting with deep-trench edging. To create this edge, use a sharp square-point shovel or spade to dig into sod 4 inches away from the planting bed. Dig 4–6 inches deep and lift out turf, roots and all. Clear the trench of soil, roots, and rocks. Fill it with mulch for a classy look. Refresh a trench edge at least once a season to keep grass out of beds.

Over time, as funds permit, exchange the trench for a dressier touch with masonry, metal, wood, or plastic edging. Of the four materials, plastic is the least expensive and might last the shortest time. Masonry offers a pricier, more durable and permanent edge. Without mortar in joints, bricks and pavers do permit grass, perennials, and weeds to grow between them. Choose a masonry type that complements your home's exterior for a coordinated, formal look.

For whimsical shapes and peekaboo charm, look for intricately patterned aluminum, wrought-iron, or steel border fences that promise strength and enduring quality. Wrought iron and steel benefit from an antirust treatment for greatest durability. Metal is a wonderful choice for a formal or traditional-style garden.

Wood edging might be crafted from bamboo, willow, or other woods and can be counted on to enhance a garden's cottage or Asian ambience. Wood in contact with soil will decompose at some point; plan to replace edging over time.

Edge the edging

No matter what edging you use, create a mowing strip so you can easily maneuver the mower alongside the edging. Clear a shallow trench to accommodate mower wheels, or lay down a strip of mulch or recycled-rubber mulch. Without a mowing strip, you'll have to string-trim every bed.

Care
Watering & Irrigation

Adequate hydration is vital to the success of any plant. It's especially important right after planting.

Water is vital to plant health, moving through plants from roots to leaves. As water travels through a perennial, it carries nutrients from the soil to growing leaves. When water evaporates from leaves, it acts as a cooling mechanism, like sweat on a person.

Irrigation frequency

Watering perennials can be tricky, because plants show the same symptoms when they're suffering from overwatering or underwatering. The most accurate way to know whether plants need water is to check the soil. If it's wet 3–4 inches deep, you don't need to water. Check soil moisture in several locations in the garden, because each area might dry out at different rates.

Water perennials infrequently and deeply. This means applying water for a longer period instead of a quick pass with a garden hose. Morning is the best time of day to water. You can deliver water to your garden using soaker hoses, drip irrigation, an overhead sprinkler, or by hand. Some gardeners prefer to water by hand, using that time to inspect plants; others like an automated system. If you use automatic irrigation, make sure you can override any programmed settings so plants aren't overwatered during rainy spells.

How much water?

A guideline for watering established perennials is to provide ½–1½ inches of water per week in summer, delivered through rainfall or irrigation. During spring and fall, provide that amount of water in a two-week window. In areas where the ground doesn't freeze, 1–2 inches per month is sufficient in winter.

Some perennials, such as coneflower, lavender, penstemon, and white gaura, are more drought-tolerant than others and require less water. Newly planted gardens require consistently moist soil, especially for bare-root plants or small starts.

To calibrate automated irrigation, measure how much water you're applying by setting out shallow containers marked in ½-inch increments. Track how long it takes for your irrigation system to deliver the prescribed amount of water and set timers accordingly. In some situations, you might notice that water runs off the bed before 1 inch is delivered to soil. In this case, set the irrigation system to cycle off for 30 minutes after it hits the point of runoff.

How do you know when you have watered enough? Measure the water applied, or for a more accurate gauge, soak the first 8 inches of soil. That's the goal of deep watering, which encourages deep roots. An easy test to determine whether the soil is soaked is to insert a screwdriver into the planting bed. In moist soil, the blade will slip in easily.

WATER WISDOM

Make the most of the water you use in your garden by adopting conservation practices. Here are six simple water-saving techniques.

Apply mulch. A mulch layer slows water evaporation from the soil surface.

Avoid wind. Don't use overhead watering on windy days.

Water early. Water early in the day, when wind speed and temperature are lower, to reduce evaporation losses.

Group like plants. Arrange plants in the garden by water needs. Group perennials that need water during dry periods, and scatter drought-tolerant ones throughout the rest of the garden.

Use microclimates. Plant water-loving perennials near downspouts and hard surfaces, where runoff tends to douse soil.

Water roots. Use soaker hoses or drip irrigation to deliver water directly to roots and eliminate evaporation that can occur during overhead sprinkling.

Care
Fertilizing & Nutrition

Feeding your landscape plantings will make them perform better. That means more growth, better flower production, and increased vigor.

Most plants find and absorb adequate nutrients from soil, with the exception of nitrogen (N), phosphorus (P), and potassium (K). These are the nutrients most commonly added in the form of fertilizer. Fertilizer labels indicate the percentage of the three nutrients as a series of numbers, such as 15-30-15, which indicates that 15 percent of the weight of the bag is nitrogen, another 15 percent is potassium, and 30 percent is phosphorus.

Types of fertilizer

Organic fertilizers, such as manures and compost, have low levels of nutrients but improve soil structure, favor a healthy population of soil microbes and worms, and contribute micronutrients plants need. Manures are also bulky, vary in nutrient concentration, and require a large quantity to deliver an adequate amount of nutrients. Some organic fertilizers, such as blood meal, bonemeal, and cottonseed meal, are more concentrated, so a smaller amount is required. Most meal fertilizers require microbes to break them down.

Soluble fertilizers, when dissolved in water, deliver a quick nutrient burst to plants. They're easy to handle and often contain a high percentage of nutrients per weight. Controlled-release fertilizers discharge nutrients gradually over time. These products can be more expensive, but they provide a steady nutrient source that can feed plants up to an entire growing season. They don't improve the soil like manure. If you don't amend the soil with specific nutrients when planting, feed newly planted perennials.

Fertilizer application methods

With organic and inorganic fertilizers, you'll scatter the material over the soil surface. The method depends on the fertilizer you choose: liquid blends or granular types.

Liquid blends

With water-soluble fertilizers, use either a watering can or a hose-end sprayer. Make sure the solution is properly and thoroughly mixed. Distribute the mixture directly onto the soil around plants. If you're dealing with a foliar fertilizer, such as kelp or fish emulsion, follow label instructions carefully. Avoid applying liquid fertilizers to soil that's bone-dry; the salts in fertilizers can burn roots. Wet the soil first, then pour on the fertilizer. Don't apply liquid fertilizers before forecast rain.

Granular types

Uncoated granules release nutrients rapidly; they're sometimes called fast-release plant food. Their quick nutrient release is triggered by moisture. Even the moisture from your hands will release the nutrients. If you apply uncoated fast-release granules with bare hands, you'll experience stinging if you have any cuts, and the granules will wick moisture from your hands, so it's best to wear gloves when applying. When using uncoated granular fertilizer, you'll need to reapply the product more frequently.

Prilled granular fertilizers have a specialized coating designed to break down slowly and release nutrients at a constant rate. The longevity of the fertilizer will vary from one to nine months.

To apply granular fertilizers, scatter the product over the soil surface around plants, sprinkling it in a ring about 6 inches beyond the outer edge of the broadest point. Scratch the fertilizer into the soil, covering the granules. Take care not to let fertilizer fall into the crowns of perennials, touching foliage. This is especially important with fast-release fertilizer granules, which can burn leaves. If fertilizer gets on leaves, wash it off.

With a bed that's mulched, pull the mulch back, apply the fertilizer, and replace the mulch. Water in the fertilizer after applying or time your application just before rainfall.

IT'S ALL ABOUT TIMING

The ideal time to apply fertilizer is just before episodes of active growth.

In wintry regions, fertilize in early spring as plants are beginning to poke through the soil. Spring rains will keep the soil moist and nutrients available to actively growing roots.

In the mildest climes, aim for a late-autumn application, so fertilizer is available to roots in moist winter soil.

With container perennials, time applications as indicated above. Or opt to use water-soluble fertilizer applied every two to four weeks during the growing season.

Avoid applying liquid fertilizer to soil just before a rainfall, which can leach nutrients quickly through the soil.

right After setting a perennial into soil, begin to backfill the planting hole, tamping soil into the empty spaces. When the soil is even with the surrounding bed, add mulch.

Care
Mulching

When choosing mulch, you want a natural-looking material that doesn't rob nutrients from the soil.

Some mulches, such as wood chips, sawdust, and straw, draw nitrogen out of the soil as they decay, which can cause nutrient issues for plants. If possible, use wood-based mulches that are well-rotted or take longer to decompose, such as high-quality shredded hardwood bark. When you must use a wood-based mulch that's not decomposed, add a slow-release fertilizer to the soil surface before applying the mulch.

Some mulches offer greater longevity than others. Grass clippings and spoiled hay last a few weeks to a few months; cocoa hulls, pine straw, and fresh wood chips last one to three years. If you tap into a locally available compost source, such as seaweed, spent mushroom soil, or chopped leaves, you'll spend little to nothing on mulch.

Spent Mushroom Soil
Risk of weed seeds: No

Nitrogen impact: None

Availability: Very local

Cost: Free to inexpensive

Durability: Several months to a year

Comments: Adds organic matter but not significant amounts of nutrients.

Cottonseed Hulls
Risk of weed seeds: No

Nitrogen impact: None

Availability: Very local

Cost: Free to inexpensive

Durability: Several months to a year

Comments: Might be blown away in windy areas.

Fresh Wood Chips
Risk of weed seeds: No

Nitrogen impact: Severe

Availability: Widespread

Cost: Free or inexpensive

Durability: 1–4 years

Comments: Use after composting.

Sawdust
Risk of weed seeds: No

Nitrogen impact: Severe

Availability: Local to regional

Cost: Free or inexpensive

Durability: 1–3 years

Comments: Use only after several years of decomposition: Do not use sawdust from treated wood.

Salt-Marsh Hay
Risk of weed seeds: No

Nitrogen impact: Limited

Availability: Local to regional

Cost: Moderate

Durability: 1 year

Comments: Some concern about environmental impact of harvesting.

Shredded Cypress
Risk of weed seeds: No

Nitrogen impact: Limited

Availability: Widespread

Cost: Moderate

Durability: More than 5 years

Comments: More durable than most mulches but less beneficial to soil.

Pine Straw

Risk of weed seeds: No

Nitrogen impact: Slight

Availability: Local to regional

Cost: Inexpensive to moderate

Durability: 1–2 years

Comments: Might be blown away in windy areas.

Cocoa Hulls

Risk of weed seeds: No

Nitrogen impact: None

Availability: Widespread

Cost: Expensive

Durability: 1–3 years

Comments: Deliciously fragrant.

Shredded Hardwood

Risk of weed seeds: No

Nitrogen impact: Limited

Availability: Widespread

Cost: Moderate

Durability: 1–3 years

Comments: In recent years quality has declined and might vary widely.

Shredded Pine Bark

Risk of weed seeds: No

Nitrogen impact: Limited

Availability: Widespread

Cost: Moderate

Durability: 1–3 years

Comments: Use instead of pine nuggets, which can tie up nitrogen.

Straw

Risk of weed seeds: Yes

Nitrogen impact: Slight

Availability: Widespread

Cost: Inexpensive

Durability: 1 year

Comments: Keep bales wet for several weeks to germinate all seeds before applying.

Chopped Leaves

Risk of weed seeds: No

Nitrogen impact: Slight

Availability: Widespread

Cost: Free or inexpensive

Durability: 1 year or less

Comments: Best if partially decomposed.

Municipal Compost

Risk of weed seeds: Yes

Nitrogen impact: None

Availability: Local, most often in urban and suburban areas

Cost: Free or inexpensive

Durability: 1 year or less

Comments: Quality varies significantly, depending on the municipality.

Packaged Compost

Risk of weed seeds: No

Nitrogen impact: None

Availability: Widespread

Cost: Expensive

Durability: Several months

Comments: Better used as a soil additive than a mulch.

Care
Staking & Training

Some plants require hidden infrastructure in the form of staking to help them grow correctly and stay upright.

The key to garden beauty lies largely unseen. Showy bloomers and striking foliage command attention, but it's well-amended soil, compost, mulch, and nutrients that invisibly fuel the show. In the same way, stakes and supports create a hidden infrastructure that keeps a garden looking its best.

The case for stakes

Perennials lean, topple, and flop for a variety of reasons. Sometimes an otherwise sturdy stem tumbles when rain and wind conspire with weighty blooms to bend stems to the ground. In other cases, stems grow lush and weak because of overfertilizing; most established perennials thrive on limited fertilizer. A mulch of compost in spring or an annual addition of an organic fertilizer scratched into soil power plentiful growth without creating weak stems.

Sun-loving plants in part shade tend to stretch for the sun and frequently require staking. Other perennials are simply more prone to flop by virtue of large flower heads or lanky stems.

In their natural habitat, many perennials don't require staking because they grow among—and lean on—taller, stronger plants, such as grasses, shrubs, or bushy perennials. Tackle leaning and falling stems by emulating nature's planting schemes in your garden, or craft your own system of stakes and supports.

Stake them up

Staking typically falls into two categories: preventive and remedial. Preventive staking involves thoughtful planning and action before stems collapse. It's what you do for known floppers in your garden, such as peonies and meadow rue.

Choose from a variety of stakes to support perennials. Grow-through supports work well with plants that tend to flop just before bloom, such as aster, boltonia, garden phlox, and goldenrod. Select plastic-coated wire cages, tomato cages, or grids for grow-through supports. Grid stakes offer sturdy support for heavy-headed bloomers and multistem perennials, such as peony, false indigo, Russian sage, and tall daisies. You can also use tree and shrub prunings, branches that blow down from trees, or even boughs cut from discarded Christmas trees (after needles fall off).

With preventive staking, insert supports in spring, when plants are emerging from soil. This is vitally important for grow-through and grid stakes. As plants grow, stems weave through stakes, effectively absorbing them into the clump and hiding them from view.

Remedial staking is reactive, inserting supports after perennials fall over because of high winds, strong summer downpours, or other interference. Keep a variety of materials on hand to make supports—twine, plant ties, bamboo stakes, single stakes, and branched twigs.

In general, when you stake, you want the support to fall somewhere between the midpoint of plant height and the peak growing point. That's easy to judge with remedial staking. With preventive staking, choose supports based on final plant height.

Unleash your creative instincts and invent your own staking system using straight stakes, string, linking stakes, tomato cages, chicken wire, twine—whatever you have on hand. Approach your staking ideas with a trial-and-error attitude. If something doesn't work for one perennial, it might for another. You'll find the best solution as you continue crafting.

Tomato cages

Versatile and inexpensive, tomato cages can fill many roles in a garden and landscape. Press extra-large ones (3–4 feet tall) into service supporting tall, bushy bloomers such as Joe Pye weed, hollyhock, and meadow rue. Medium-size cages (2–3 feet tall) graciously corral midrange perennials such as peach-leaf bellflower, purple coneflower, and Siberian iris. Transform a tomato cage into a grow-through support by wrapping and weaving twine across the horizontal support wires to form a loose grid.

Use bolt cutters to transform cages into cut-to-size supports. Snip tomato cage legs just above hoops to form stakes of varying heights. For perennials growing along a fence or wall, clip cages at one spot along the hoop on each horizontal circle then open the cage to form a half-circle support.

Bamboo and twine

Combine stakes and twine to craft custom supports that you adapt and complete during the growing season. Insert stakes in early spring before plants need them. Drive the stakes deep into the soil to anchor them.

As perennial stems emerge, tie twine around one stake and string it to the next stake, looping it around that stake a few times before continuing to the next stake. Add string layers throughout the growing season as stems continue to soar skyward. Keep the string tight enough to support leaning stems but loose enough to prevent a trussed-up look.

At the end of the growing season, remove this support when you clean up the garden. Wooden and bamboo stakes slowly rot over time, so it's wise to remove them from the soil over winter. Dipping the ends of wooden supports in wax can help slow the deterioration process.

Chicken wire

Form chicken wire into a cage that's slightly narrower than the mature width of the floppy perennial you want to coax upright. Place the wire cylinder against soil, and anchor it by weaving bamboo stakes through the wire into the soil. This is a wonderful choice for bushlike perennials that have thin stems, such as aster, baby's breath, helenium, or plants that rabbits tend to nibble.

PLANTS THAT NEED STAKING

No matter how perfect your growing conditions, some perennials just tend to lean and benefit from a little extra support from one or more stake types.

1. ASTER Grid, grow-through, tomato cage
2. BALLOON FLOWER Grid, grow-through, tomato cage, twig stake
3. BOLTONIA Grow-through, tomato cage, twig stake
4. CENTRANTHUS Grow-through, tomato cage, twig stake
5. FOXGLOVE Single stake
6. GAYFEATHER Hoop, tomato cage, twig stake
7. GOLDENROD Grow-through, tomato cage
8. DELPHINIUM Single stake
9. HELENIUM Grow-through, tomato cage
10. PEONY Grid, grow-through, tomato cage

Care: Staking & Training

Ways to support plants

There are as many ways to support plants as there are creative gardeners. Shown here are a collection of some favorite kinds of supports that are commercially available, as well as some traditional techniques.

STAKING SUPPLIES

Stock your toolshed with a variety of plant stakes and materials you can cobble together to create plant supports. Use this list to get started.

STAKING GEAR

Bamboo straight stakes	Grow-through stakes
Bamboo U-stakes	Padded wire
Bolt cutters	Plant ties
Chicken wire	Tomato cages
Cotton string	Twine
Grid stakes	

left Plants such as Oriental lilies require individual stakes for individual stems. Metal spiral stakes offer function with artistic style.

Grid

Flat, circular grid with three or four legs; push legs into soil first, then snap ring in place; stems grow through grid.

USE WITH clump-forming perennials, such as peony, garden phlox, sea holly, monkshood.

Grow-Through

Flat, circular support with concentric circles; three or four legs push into soil; stems grow through circles.

USE WITH multistem, upright plants with thin stems, such as balloon flower, blanket flower, bugbane, helenium.

Linking

Upright pieces with arms that link and form joints you can bend.

USE WITH any perennial that has flopped, is overtaking less-vigorous plants, or is leaning into a path. Examples are centranthus, crocosmia, pincushion flower, ladybells, Shasta daisy.

Mesh Cage

Form a cylinder of chicken wire slightly narrower than the mature width of the plant you're staking; place it over the perennial early in the season; thread a few stakes through the mesh; sink into soil for added support.

USE WITH sprawling perennials such as aster, blackberry lily, obedient plant, yarrow.

Other Plants

Position floppy perennials near stronger perennial or shrub neighbors, and let stems lean on those plants for support.

USE WITH all perennials.

Single Stake

Use twine, hook-and-loop plant ties, or padded wire to bind stems to bamboo or wood stakes; look for single-stem stakes at garden centers.

USE WITH tall perennials topped with heavy flower spikes, such as delphinium, foxglove, hollyhock, lily.

Tomato Cage

Sink a tomato cage into soil; thread a few stakes through cage sides and sink into soil for added support.

USE WITH clump-forming perennials, such as helenium, salvia, showy sedum.

Twig Stake

Insert sturdy branched twigs into soil near floppy plants for support.

USE WITH clump-forming perennials, such as false sunflower, meadow sage, spotted bellflower.

CHAPTER FIVE

Dream Landscapes Gallery

Beautiful, well-designed landscapes offer inspiration for your own yard and garden.

Edible Landscaping

Accessorized with flowers and herbs, a vegetable garden can be as beautiful as it is bountiful.

Imagine making a healthful meal from the produce raised organically in your own backyard. That's what the owners of this property in Southern California were able to do by creating a landscape that is as beautiful as it is tasty. They made the most of their small lot by combining their favorite edibles and flowers to create a pretty and productive outdoor escape.

Edible landscaping is a trend that is growing in popularity, because what is more appealing that stepping out your door to collect berries for breakfast or herbs for a pasta sauce? Interplanting vegetables, fruits, and herbs into both front and backyard landscapes and inside traditional flower garden beds means that the area surrounding your home can be more than just beautiful; it can be productive, nutritious, and delicious.

Weeds don't stand a chance in this action-packed landscape— there simply isn't space. The star of the landscape is a fruit and vegetable garden decorated with flowering plants. Tucked into a small plateau on the side of a hill, the diversity of the mixed plantings adds to the spectacular view and promotes organic gardening techniques. Some plants, such as Queen Anne's lace and dill, attract beneficial insects, while marigolds, onions, and garlic repel bad bugs, contributing to a pesticide-free garden.

Orderly raised beds contain the vigorous plants. The frames hold quick-draining soil that is friendly to the roots of most edibles. Easy-to-grow annual and perennial flowers planted in inviting drifts help secure the hillside. The plants also mingle among the steps leading to the vegetable garden and color the landscape year-round.

opposite A rail fence frames the potager, or kitchen garden. *right* Succulent strawberries in a pot on a metal stand are within easy grasp for sampling.

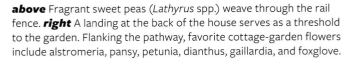

above Fragrant sweet peas (*Lathyrus* spp.) weave through the rail fence. **right** A landing at the back of the house serves as a threshold to the garden. Flanking the pathway, favorite cottage-garden flowers include alstromeria, pansy, petunia, dianthus, gaillardia, and foxglove.

If you already grow plants in your yard, it will be easy to incorporate vegetables, fruits, and herbs into your existing beds to make your landscape edible. Adding plants that produce food to your landscape is not labor-intensive or complicated. Just use vegetable, fruit, and herb plants in the same way you'd use other plantings. For example, edge a walkway with low-growing alpine strawberries, or tuck colorful tricolor sage amid flowers in a border. Frilly-leaf kale makes gorgeous container plants that can be clipped for dinner. Even greens such as lettuces make beautiful additions to window boxes or sunny porch planters, especially when they are just steps away from the kitchen for easy mealtime access.

To design an edible landscape, first take stock of your yard. Look for lackluster plants you can replace with varieties that have edible features. For example, blueberries, with their spring flowers, tasty fruits, and exceptional fall color, make ideal hedge plants. Also consider growing fruit or nut trees. Locate them away from driveways, patios, decks, and walkways so the inevitable fruit and nut drop doesn't cause a mess. If you're lacking space, check out columnar varieties of apples that grow taller than they are wide. Some varieties will also excel in containers.

Most edibles perform best in locations that receive six to eight hours of full sun each day. Cool-season plants, such as lettuce, spinach, radishes, and cabbage, can tolerate some shade. Garden structures such as obelisks and trellises add interest to your landscape and can support vining edibles such as peas or squash. You can even dress up tomato cages in bright paint colors and add them as structural features of your landscape.

Finally, remember that you don't need to grow edibles in straight, boring rows, like a traditional produce garden. Be creative. Plant in graphic, pleasing patterns, leaving enough space between plants to avoid overcrowding but close enough to create a dense appearance and shade out weeds. When annual vegetables, such as peppers or tomatoes, are done producing, they can be pulled out of the landscape and added to the compost pile.

opposite Sweet peas climb the garden fence while a crazy quilt of annuals, herbs, and perennials clambers up the hillside, adding beauty in waves of color throughout the season. **right** Although this backyard vegetable garden sits on a slope, it's readily accessible just steps from the house and kitchen.

Colorful Entryways

An Atlanta cottage comes alive when a color-rich garden replaces a tired front lawn.

Gardening in a front yard has so many advantages, it's a wonder that most gardens are hidden behind the house. Think curb appeal: A lush garden is a beautiful way to enhance the front of a house, making it a standout in the neighborhood. Plus, front yards often lack play structures, pools, and other gardening obstacles. So what better way is there to greet a guest to your home than with a colorful perennial garden?

Once a dull expanse of turf and a few foundation shrubs, this front yard in Atlanta no longer has a lawn at all. The grass was removed, and in its place grows a horticultural symphony of color and texture. The homeowner can now spend time enjoying the view and smelling the flowers instead of participating in a rigorous all-summer mowing schedule.

The garden's tidy white picket fence and formal walkways are accented by cottage-style planting beds where the plants mingle freely. The full-sun planting beds are packed with hundreds of annuals, perennials, and shrubs.

This Southern garden has a traditional design based on a line drawn from the street to the front door, providing a straight shot to the entry, as well as the framework for a foursquare plan. The primary paths that form the main axes are paved with old bricks. Secondary paths are carpeted with pea gravel for contrast and a cottage-garden feel.

Symmetry reigns supreme in this garden, lending a sense of formal order to the boisterous plantings. Four main beds are created by intersecting walkways. Each bed is anchored in its center by a tree-form hydrangea. Beyond the foursquare planting beds are rectangular plots offering additional space for pass-along plants that the homeowner gathered from her mother's and grandmother's gardens.

opposite This Atlanta home's location on a corner lot accommodates an updated landscape design with front and side entries from public sidewalks. **right** A straight path leads directly from the street to the front door of the painted-brick cottage. Before a single brick could be laid in the walkway, the old lawn had to be torn out.

The garden contains many old-fashioned flower favorites, such as snapdragon, larkspur, and clematis. Several types of annual plants self-seed and eventually pop up all over the garden. Extra seedlings are easy to pluck out where they are not wanted, but those that remain add to the garden's cottage charm and lush appearance.

The crowded community of plantings is by design. It looks beautiful yet has utilitarian purpose. Shoulder-to-shoulder plantings mean there's less chance that weeds can pop up, invade, and take over. A layer of mulch added in the early spring before perennials gain height can reduce the weeding chores of this all-yard garden to nearly nil.

Window boxes raise the garden's profile and add spots of color to the landscape, as well as connect the garden's bounty to the house. Matched containers planted with standards bring the formality of the garden right up to the front door.

Mixing elements of formality and informality in a landscape is easy and attractive. The formal elements of this landscape include the foursquare design and boxwood balls edging the front garden. But the homeowner's love of color and excess is achieved with the wild mix of perennials and annuals that grows within the outlined boundaries, a decidedly informal element.

Another benefit of an all-flower front yard is the seasonal show of color and texture. With a mix of perennials, bulbs, and annuals, there is a constantly changing flower show as the seasons unfold. Spring-flowering bulbs, such as narcissus, with early-spring perennials, such as hellebore, open the gardening season. Colorful summer perennials, such as iris, foxglove, and daylily, add bright spots to the landscape during the hottest months. Evergreen plantings, such as boxwood, offer color and structure during the winter months.

Planning an all-front-yard flowering landscape is a bold move. For the right home and gardener, it may be the best way to enjoy an Eden-like landscape in all seasons.

opposite The front yard is a four-square garden formed by intersecting walkways. Secondary gravel paths strike an informal balance. **right** Ivy follows the curves of the concrete steps, while wrought-iron railings shape a wide welcome at the front entry.

opposite The cottage-style garden gains its picturesque charm from picket fencing, gates, and stacked-stone pillars. Plants benefit from well-amended soil and drip irrigation. **above** Larkspur, snapdragon, and hollyhock are among the old-fashioned flowers that line the garden paths and reseed themselves each year.

Backyard Bliss

At this Silicon Valley home, the pool and garden brim with beauty for the whole family.

Designing a backyard that is welcoming to groups of both giggling grade-schoolers and business associates is a tall order. This California landscape meets the challenge with style, thanks to a few special features.

Surrounded by travertine limestone—the same stone used to build retaining walls on the site—the pool splashes with excitement when the five fountains bubble forth from the walls backing the oasis. Turn off the fountains, and the pool becomes a meditative reflecting pond. Nearby, stately stucco columns support a wisteria-clad pergola, adding to the classic style of the backyard.

The pool area feels secluded because the pergola is planted with flowering vines. The garden area planted around the pool is packed tightly with perennial plants for year-round beauty. It's important to choose non-shedding types of plants for landscaping around pools so plant debris doesn't pose a problem for the filtration system.

Barely visible from the pool area is a dream destination for young visitors—a two-story castle complete with turrets, bridges, a tube slide, and swings. Partially masked by a dense planting of fruit trees, this luxurious play area is close enough to the main gathering area that the children can be easily monitored, but far enough away that they feel like they are in their own piece of paradise.

The play area is surrounded by perennial gardens that require little attention; plants come back each spring and create a season-long magical garden of bloom. It's the perfect setting for the family's kids and pets.

opposite This soothing setting blends the pool with a pergola overhead and surrounding patio, walls, and fountains. The outdoor living area suits the contemporary house. *right* The path to the kids' castle leads through a wildflower meadow to an orchard. The turreted playhouse stands as a treasure trove of fun.

above A pool topped the list of priorities for the homeowners when they worked with a landscape architect. Now the family flocks daily to their backyard retreat, where the pool draws guests of all ages. **left** Concrete steppers border one side of the pool and extend beyond it, linking the outdoor living area with the dwelling. The clean lines and careful geometry work with the modern architecture of the house. **opposite** On the hillside between the children's play structure and the formal pool area, there's room to run wild. The lawn and relaxed perennial plantings blend the landscape's activity areas.

Living Large

Garden structures big and small create mini destinations in a narrow suburban yard.

Turn big garden dreams into reality on a small plot of land by incorporating a variety of garden structures. Defined by a pergola, a fence, and an arbor, the garden rooms on this narrow lot in suburban Chicago live much larger than their dimensions.

Designed to be a series of destinations, the 60-foot-wide landscape includes a patio, dining pergola, pond garden, and cutting garden. A large honey locust tree holds court near the back porch and shades the checkerboard patio made of pavers and grass. A short stretch of picket fence, painted white to partner with the house, defines one edge of the space while a flagstone walkway defines the opposite side.

The flagstone path leads the way to a magnificent white pergola covered with grapevines and supported by classic white columns. Nestled against the garage, the pergola offers views of the landscape from the cozy confines of a garden room. Around the corner from the pergola and behind the garage is the cutting garden, divided into formal raised squares and surrounded by a pea-gravel walk. Geometric trellises, as well as another white fence, define this area of the landscape.

At the far end of the lot, waterlilies bloom just above the shiny black surface of the garden pond. With the pond partially hidden by flowering perennials and shrubs, finding it is like discovering a garden treasure. Details such as this make the space feel larger.

The numerous garden rooms on the small lot had the potential to feel chaotic, but everything is held together in pleasing harmony due to careful use of coordinated color and accents. A simple black-and-white color scheme unites the garden structures, and white birdhouses are the main accents.

opposite Inspired by the style of grand Southern gardens, the homeowners laid a straight path of salvaged bricks from the street to the front door. Low wrought-iron fencing begins the array of tidy details. *right* Updating the home's exterior began with painting the brick white and adding black shutters. This also provided a color palette for the garden structures to come.

The structural assets of this landscape created numerous places within the yard, each with a distinct sense of style and place. A pergola swathed with blooming roses creates a bower of bloom over a dining table. The formal garden features a classic garden and bricked bed, backed by a white fence with a bevy of purple martin houses. A white picket fence and another collection of birdhouses create a cozy corner in the yard.

Tucked among evergreens and other trees or positioned in the middle of the yard, a pergola can match the style of your home, or deviate from it. While pergolas are generally free standing, they also work well with other structures, such as a garage or attached to a house.

Perhaps the largest of outdoor structures, a pergola is an ideal way to add an outdoor room to a backyard. Do you need additional outdoor dining space? A pergola covering a dining table can create a shaded haven for meals.

Pergolas can also offer a respite from the sun. If your yard is awash in sunshine, a pergola can provide a shaded spot to cool down on a hot, sunny day. The shade from a backyard structure can also offer a different gardening venue; it's a spot where shade-craving plants, such as hostas or begonias, can thrive in containers or planted in the ground.

above left Adding a pergola along one side of the garage created a room for outdoor entertaining. With a canopy of 'William Baffin' roses and grapevines overhead, it provides a cool, shaded nook in the mostly sunny yard. **left** White adirondack chairs with crisp white-and-blue cushions offer comfortable seating. **opposite above** A 24 × 24-foot area behind the garage features a formally arranged cutting garden and a potting bench. Lattice gives the garden walls a finished look. **opposite, below left** The confines of the 60-foot-wide backyard include the garage and a large garden room with various small, inviting areas. The homeowners used a garden hose to lay out the garden beds, eventually making them twice the size they first envisioned. **opposite, below right** A ready-made seat arbor proved too small for the space, so the homeowner hired a carpenter to add a larger arch and the lattice back with oval cutout. She discovered that outdoor furnishings needed to be bigger than she thought.

Diamond patterns throughout the garden add unity. Under the backyard's mature honey locust tree, precast exposed-aggregate stepping-stones are set at an angle and separated by strips of grass to form a dramatic patio with the appearance of latticework.

Low-Maintenance Landscape

Angular lines, plant repetition, and concrete blocks create the bones of an inviting, modern California landscape.

Designing a garden to complement the house is always a winning strategy. If your house has a modern flavor, take cues from this well-done contemporary landscape.

Concrete blocks set the tone for this sloping yard in Ojai, California. The blocks were painted white and used to create a collection of raised planters and retaining walls. The smooth blocks match materials from the house itself, and the straight lines of the walls underscore the home's modern geometry.

The first wall that visitors see—just 8 inches high—edges a courtyard beside the driveway. Higher retaining walls create the pea-gravel terrace that stretches across one side of the house.

Accessible via a stepping-stone path and slate-tile steps, the 20 × 32-foot terrace is spacious enough for hosting parties, but it's also a tranquil and intimate retreat. The entry court's spillway is visible—and audible—from a dining area that occupies one corner. Beyond the dining terrace, a low-maintenance planting of leatherleaf sedge rustles in the breeze.

The organic materials used to make the landscape add to its simplicity as well as its easy care. Stone mulch around the beds means little or no weeding. The gravel dining area requires little care other than an occasional raking.

opposite Just off the terrace, a rooftop deck above the garage extends the outdoor living area. Burro's tail (*Sedum morganianum*) that tumbles over the edge of a planter is among the spare, easy-care plantings. **right** A spillway, added to the entry courtyard by pouring concrete to form waterproof walls, is home to a potted variegated fortnight lily (*Dietes iridioides*).

above Before the landscape makeover, the yard was a big slope; a concrete slab provided a landing outside the house. Now a courtyard entryway leads down steps to the driveway and across stepping-stones to a gravel terrace.
left A bonsai-pruned mugo pine stands out against the painted-block exterior along the front entry. Sedum fills the planting bed with uncluttered beauty.

The plantings in this minimalist landscape are suited for the region. Grasses create fountains for foliage in the dry landscape. Repetition of plant materials also creates a unified look. The plant selection is mostly green foliage plants (and nonflowering), but the landscape feels complete, concentrating on textural beauty rather than color.

Grasses are extremely useful in low-maintenance landscapes. Their upright shape and uniform growth make them excellent choices in modern gardens. Plus, grasses offer all-season interest. Ornamental grasses rarely steal the show, but their subtle beauty is never far from the limelight. From 6-inch mounds perfect for edging to towering 20-foot screens, there's a grass for every garden nook. Choose from a wide range of textures, seasonal colors, and outlines. Use their features to separate color swaths, to soften edges, and to blend boundaries.

Happily, most grasses are adaptable and a cinch to grow. In spring or fall, plant varieties suited to your local environment in soil enriched with compost. Each spring, after giving grasses a short haircut, work a low-nitrogen, slow-release fertilizer into the soil around the plants. Divide when necessary in early spring. Most will require watering only during dry spells.

Grasses reward good care with year-round beauty. Because most don't drop foliage during dormancy, they provide shape, color, texture, movement, and wind song long after frost-shy plants have finished their performances.

above right An army of sedges (tall, wispy *Carex buchananii* and low *Carex compacta*) marches across the terrace in a simple yet dramatic display. The mass planting looks good year-round. ***right*** Mexican feathergrass (*Stipa tenuissima*) fills planters along the front stairway, continuing the planting scheme's focus on simplicity. With plantings secondary to such hard elements as walls, terraces, and paths, this landscape design works well with the home's architecture.

This dining terrace with a pea-gravel floor brings a rustic, Mediterranean flavor to the high-style, low-maintenance landscape design. Terracing the hillside makes it appear larger as well as more accommodating.

Panoramic Oasis

An innovative pool and spa form the centerpiece of a backyard designed for family-friendly living.

An impressive, natural-looking pool is the heart of this backyard in Carlsbad, California, but it's the smaller design features, such as landscape lighting and poolside seating, that make the landscape a favorite destination day and night. Take cues from this landscape as you craft your own backyard paradise.

On a stiflingly hot day, the pool's beach entry provides a place for semisubmerged lounging. And at day's end, the adjoining spa offers one of the best seats in the house for watching the sunset. Boulders artfully positioned around the perimeter of the pool complement its organic shape. The stone theme continues on the bottom of the pool, which is lined with smooth black onyx pebbles.

An outdoor kitchen sits at one end of the pool and a slightly raised seating area at the other. A small stone bridge arching over a softly flowing stream provides access to the seating area, which overlooks the pool and a neighboring canyon. You're sure to stay warm on cool nights thanks to a cozy gas fireplace.

Adding outdoor features to match your interests and lifestyle makes your landscape more attractive and, of course, usable. For example, if you love to cook and entertain outdoors, an outdoor kitchen, grilling area, smoker, or brick pizza oven might be a good addition. If leisurely activities such as soaking or swimming are a family favorite, a spa or lap pool may be a better fit for your landscape. If you have only evenings to spend in your yard, a fire pit or lighted water feature might serve the purpose. Building a backyard haven where you and your family can enjoy specific likes and hobbies will mean more outdoor family time together.

right As an element of the backyard design, the pool provides proportion and balance. In addition to a built-in spa, the pool features a continuous-flow skimmer, a sonar-safety device (which detects unusual disturbances of the water's surface), and a saltwater chlorinator (which makes the water easy on eyes and skin).

left A sheltered outdoor kitchen and an umbrella-shaded sitting area overlook the pool. Shade is essential for outdoor living in Southern California, and a watering hole offers a fun, refreshing splash on hot days. *top* The backyard design focuses on destinations organized in a series of multipurpose rooms, such as a pergola-sheltered poolside sitting room complete with fireplace. *above* In the poolside garden, a stream traipses among plantings and over rocks, while its source is disguised by a tipped jar.

Fall for Color

A love of brilliant autumn leaves transforms this landscape into a symphony of color and texture every fall.

After a long gardening season, sending your landscape into winter with color-rich style is as simple as planting a few trees, shrubs, and perennials that revel in chilly autumn temperatures. This small garden in Port Townsend, Washington, celebrates fall with bold strokes of rich red, warm yellow, and glowing orange.

Small trees and shrubs add structure to the landscape year-round and erupt with color in fall. Japanese maples—prized for their open habit, delicate texture, and fiery fall color—anchor island planting beds and cast dappled shade onto the patio. Perennial plants known for late-season color, such as tall sedum, aster, and ornamental grasses, create a colorful carpet under the small trees. A few small, slow-growing evergreens in shades ranging from blue to gold add texture and color to the garden throughout the year.

Trees can set the landscape afire each autumn when leaves turn from summer hues of green to flaming hues of red, yellow, and orange. To enjoy this golden season in your yard, plant species that are celebrated for their colorful fall foliage. American folklore credits Jack Frost for autumn foliage color. But this cold mythical character spoils the show by killing the leaf cells that produce bright hues. The truth is, nature stages the brilliant fall act to prepare trees for winter.

Autumn's shorter days signal trees to stop manufacturing chlorophyll, the dominant green pigment in leaves during spring and summer. When chlorophyll weakens, other pigments, such as carotin and anthocyanin, reveal their blazing colors.

Carotin is responsible for bright yellow and orange autumn hues. Sugar maple, birch, ash, ginkgo, redbud, beech, hickory, butternut, honey locust, linden, pecan, poplar, tuliptree, and walnut offer golden-yellow foliage each fall. For orange foliage, look for yellowwood, Ohio buckeye, and paperbark maple.

opposite Autumn brings out the best colors in this garden. It has been planted for a particularly showy year-end display. **right** A focus on foliage leads any garden to a long season of sustained color. Ornamental grasses offer aesthetic appeal year-round.

above Think big—trees and shrubs—when planning for glorious landscape views. Most of this garden's trees are deciduous. Their leaves turn color in fall and drop, allowing winter light through their branches. *right* Apples provide one more reason to look forward to fall. An espaliered apple tree, trained to the side of the house, keeps fresh fruit within easy reach.

left The garden's small trees were chosen for their vibrant autumn displays, such as the crimson coats worn by Japanese maples. The homeowner did not want to plant trees that would grow large and overwhelm the yard or cast deep shade over perennial planting areas.
above Pots hold the interesting details of rex begonia 'Escargot', grassy 'Toffee Twist' sedge, and sedum under an 'Atrolineare' Japanese maple.

Modern Marvel

A contemporary-style landscape blends sophistication (and textural plantings) with family-friendly features.

Blending the clean lines and sometimes stark features of a modern home with the curvaceous silhouettes of the outdoors can be challenging, but take heart. You have valuable tools at your disposal for mediating the tension between geometric forms and Mother Nature's rambling ways: carefully chosen and thoughtfully placed plants.

Built in 1948, this West Los Angeles home is midcentury modern with soaring ceilings, walls of windows, and angular lines. The 5,000-square-foot backyard was a jumble of concrete and overgrown plants when a young family moved in several years ago. With the help of a landscape architect, they created a space that is fun and functional and that perfectly complements the architectural style of their home.

The rectangular yard was broken up into a series of circular outdoor rooms enhanced by plants suited to the home's simplicity and the area's Zone 10 climate. New concrete pathways skirt outdoor sitting and dining areas and serve as highways for children's bikes, trikes, and scooters. A 50-foot circle of lawn offers a soft play space, and the far corner of the yard is home to a play structure with a modern twist.

The hardscape and the home's architecture make an ideal backdrop for plants with bold, geometric forms. Drifts of fuzzy yellow kangaroo paws mingle with the bold upright leaves of New Zealand flax and graceful ornamental grasses. Unlike a cottage border, which contains many different plants, the planting beds throughout this modern-style backyard consist of just a few different species planted en masse. The finely edited plant palette makes a bold statement, complementing the strong lines of the house.

opposite Large concrete slabs that once divided the backyard were replaced with a smooth, sleek-lined patio. It extends into broad walkways that serve as thoroughfares for young ones on wheels. **right** Strappy New Zealand flax (*Phormium tenax* 'Maori Queen') and yellow kangaroo paws screen the backyard sitting area that features a fire pit—a wide, shallow cast-concrete bowl from a garden supply shop.

left The selection of landscape plants includes a rich array of colors, textures, dramatic forms, and drought tolerance. *above* Papyrus prefers rich soil and submerged roots but will get by on minimal irrigation once established in Zones 10–12. It typical reaches 3–4 feet, adding vertical interest. *opposit* Salvaged round stepping-stones dot a gravel path that curves around part of a circular lawn area.

opposite Even the children's play structure has midcentury modern styling, with its angular profile and coloring. It incorporates low-maintenance composite decking and recycled-tire mulch. **above** Modern chairs outfit a sitting area at one end of the patio. The homeowner found the chairs, designed in the early 1950s by Harry Bertoia, at a flea market. **right** Giant timber bamboo (*Bambusa oldhamii*) is a clumping variety considered noninvasive. It makes a dense, leafy screen in Zones 8–11.
far right The front yard's plant palette includes drifts of kangaroo paws and blue American agave. Prickly agave is not kid-friendly, so it grows only in the steep front yard.

191

Plant for Privacy

Surrounding your place with plants creates a secluded retreat.

Creating privacy on your plot is as simple as planting a buffer. You can restrict the view and muffle sounds of street traffic or neighbors with simple plantings. That's what the homeowners did in this yard near Raleigh, North Carolina. A grove of trees, a swath of shrubs, and a bevy of flowering plants offer a beautiful barrier between outdoor living spaces and the hustle and bustle of the outside world. A wraparound fence of view-blocking vegetation provides privacy and fabulous views on three sides of this property near downtown.

The landscape reaps the benefits of seasonal color with flowers in the spring and dense green in the winter. The perimeter of the yard is almost impenetrable from view in summer. Tall shade trees, smaller ornamental trees, shrubs of all sizes, perennials, and groundcovers work together to form a dense wall that masks both views of the surrounding streets and their traffic sounds. In winter, when deciduous plants lose their leaves, broadleaf evergreens such as rhododendrons, camellias, wax myrtle, and boxwood form a green screen.

Gently curving garden beds create islands of color in the sea of green grass inside the living fence. Bold strokes of annuals, visible from the house and outdoor gathering areas, decorate the private Eden for weeks during the summer months. The beds in the interior of the yard feature plants of varying heights to create visual interest. The organization and placement of the beds of blooms also form distinct areas inside the yard, making it feel more spacious. Separate seating and dining areas create a sense of multiple rooms within the green space.

right Cheerful annuals, such as zinnia, scarlet sage, and melampodium, that endure Raleigh's sultry summers, have become the garden's workhorses. They fill in between ornamental grasses and other perennials.

There are many ways you can plant for privacy. One is to raise the profile of the plantings in your garden through elevation. Give your favorite plants better view-blocking power by growing them in raised beds or berms. You will be surprised at how much more secluded your yard feels by mounding the soil enough to add a foot or two to plant height. Plus, planting in slightly elevated spaces places medium-size plants at eye level.

Another way to add seclusion to a landscape is to grow trees, shrubs, and perennials in layers. Most people's main goal of creating a sheltered yard is to block views of neighbors. But make it an extra-secluded yard by layering plantings to form pockets where you can't see your house or another part of the yard; you'll feel like you're getting away from it all without actually going anywhere. Creating secluded areas within your yard gives you separate spaces where you can do different things. For example, when entertaining, you could serve drinks in one area and a sit-down dinner in another.

If you don't want to work on making your entire yard a private paradise, take one corner and transform it into a secluded getaway. A simple way to do this is to carefully place a couple of trees to form a pocket of seclusion; a place to enjoy your morning coffee or an after-work glass of wine.

Of course, the classic way to create a green screen is to plant a hedge. Look for evergreen varieties to provide year-round screening, or try types that lose their leaves in winter but make up for it by putting on a show with attractive flowers or a blaze of fall color. While many plants are suitable as hedges, yours will be a cinch to care for if you select a variety that's adapted to your climate and that matures at the height and width you want your hedge to be. For small areas, look for columnar types of shrubs—those that grow up rather than out. For large areas, choose wider-growing shrubs.

above left The backyard deck floats above dark pink impatiens. The view from this area sweeps across the dense border that encloses the property. **left** Tucked into the green perimeter, the garden shed keeps tools handy. A small vegetable plot sits in a sunny pocket. Teepees act as garden sculpture when not supporting pole beans or tomatoes. **opposite** Planting beds hold swaths of bright annuals, while perimeter shrubs and trees have loose, unpruned character.

left Pressure-treated wooden decking forms a clean pathway between house and garden. The walkway also gives the beds sharply defined edges—a geometric counterpoint to the plantings' exuberance.

above A gently curving path of limestone and gravel leads from the driveway to the house. It has a natural-looking and carefree presence.

English Inspiration

A spirit of traditional formality pairs with playful touches to transform a typical suburban yard into an English country garden.

Enjoying the color and form of an English garden can be as simple as traversing the gravel paths of this Seattle yard. Once home to the typical Pacific Northwest lineup of lawn, rhododendrons, junipers, and laurel hedges, the property was given new life with the help of age-old gardening traditions.

The landscape renovation began by planting a knot garden in the long, narrow strip of land behind the house. Paving stones laid in concentric circles form the floor of the garden. This arrangement sits in the center of four nearly square planting beds. Outlined in dwarf boxwood, the four beds hold lilies, Russian sage, astilbes, and hostas.

The second landscaping phase addressed privacy in the 75×200-foot side yard, which was fully exposed to the street. In keeping with the covenants of the neighborhood, a mixed border of low-growing plants creates a living screen. Oakleaf hydrangea, redtwig dogwood, and dwarf evergreen magnolia mixed with perennials to create a colorful fence.

The heart of the side-yard garden is a dining area reminiscent of a European courtyard. Filled with several inches of crushed gravel and edged with sandstone pavers, the 18×22-foot space repeats the formal lines of the knot garden. It is planted with English lavender and Japanese holly; terra-cotta urns provide corner accents. A table with six armchairs provides ample space for family meals.

A secret garden, a playful element of English garden style, is home to a secluded outdoor spa. Accessed via a recycled door painted in gold, red, and blue, the spa is tucked into a corner formed by two of the home's exterior walls and a vine-covered arbor.

opposite The arbor and raised urn form a strong focal point at the terminus of the strolling garden. To ensure a well-framed view, the urn aligns with the dining table and pathway. *right* Painted in Provençal textile colors, a recycled door and frame add privacy to the hot-tub "room."

The first step in developing a formal garden is to know the basics. Formal gardens often feature a simplistic, geometric design. Think linear when you are laying out a design. Install straight walkways or slightly curved paths made of traditional paving materials, such as brick, bluestone, pavers, or concrete, to create a sense of order and tidiness.

Repeat plant shapes and colors throughout your yard for an organized look. Plant tall lines of arborvitae as a background screen or short hedges of low-growing boxwood to edge walkways or garden beds. Create balance by mirroring plantings across a walkway or lawn. Symmetrical plantings create calming spaces that don't jar the eye. As a result, they often feel larger.

Another hallmark of formal design is simplicity, especially when it comes to plant selection. Design advice: Limit your choices. Though it can be tough to rein yourself in, choosing and sticking to a particular plant palette will reinforce the feeling of simplicity in your landscape. Select only a few different structural plants, but create impact by massing them. Do this with small perennials such as lavender or large shrubs such as hydrangea. A mass of plantings is a simple yet effective way to add color and style to a formal design.

Creating a focal point in your landscape is also key to formal design. Look through the pages of garden magazines and you'll find common focal-point elements in formal gardens: a classic column, a piece of sculpture, or a sundial. Frequently, landscape focal points are set inside a small round or square garden bed planted with low-growing annuals, perennials, or groundcovers.

Seating is also important. In nearly every formal garden, you'll find a bench or pair of chairs where one can survey the surroundings. A bench at the end of a pathway is a classic element of formal design, as well as a way to draw the eye into the garden.

opposite Arborvitae (*Thuja occidentalis* 'Emerald') planted shoulder-to-shoulder shapes a 9-foot-tall wall, and lavender encircles a terra-cotta globe in the knot garden. ***right*** Sandstone pavers were used throughout the landscape to make paths and garden edging. They combine with gravel for easy-care flooring.

left A crushed-rock floor edged with rows of Japanese holly (*Ilex crenata* 'Convexa') and English lavender (*Lavandula augustifolia*) helps give the outdoor dining room the feeling of a European courtyard. **above** Evergreen Japanese holly and aromatic lavender flank the narrow path that leads to the dining area. **opposite** A sense of order is achieved by several means. The hardscaping materials, layout, and well-defined sightlines contribute to an organized, coherent landscape design. The formal framework of this knot garden complements the relaxed strolling garden in the distance.

Leveling the Playing Field

Stone, brick, and gravel work together to create terraces for planting and play in this Oregon yard.

A slope might be the perfect terrain for a group of school kids with sleds, but it is hardly a welcoming sight when you want to create an outdoor dining room. Solve the problem of a precariously perched table and chairs with a terrace. Underutilized solutions to a common dilemma, terraces are a notable financial investment but they pay you back tenfold with improved usability of your landscape.

Terraces surround this home nestled in the hills near Portland, Oregon. After brambles were banished from the front slope, the entry was spruced up with terraced planting beds and gracious stairways that lead to a courtyard in front of the house. Paved with brick, the courtyard blends well with the brick-topped retaining walls and stairways, also constructed of brick.

Behind the house, three retaining walls support sweeping terraced areas that accommodate a house-side patio of local Camas stone, a formal boxwood parterre, and, at the base of the cleared back slope, an extensive vegetable and cutting garden.

Careful attention to detail unites the three outdoor spaces. For example, the uppermost terrace is linked to the gathering space below with a stairway that arches over a fanciful water feature. The use of brick, the dominant paving material in the front yard, continues in the back garden, where it edges the Camas stone patio. And finally, by planting in large drifts—sometimes as many as five or seven plants of the same variety—the garden seamlessly flows from one area to the next.

The terraces make way for a variety of plants, including perennials, roses, ornamental grasses, and fruits and vegetables. Water conservation was just as important in consideration of the planting palette as were lush borders. A gravel garden planted with drought-tolerant plants adds foliage and texture to the patio while reducing the water requirements in this part of the garden.

above At the back of the stucco house, an 'Autumn Sunset' rose and trumpet vine (*Campsis radicans*) clamber high above the stone patio.
opposite Terracing the backyard made way for a kitchen garden with boxwood-framed beds and pear trees espaliered against stone retaining walls.

Sloped landscapes don't have to be unusable. There is more than one way to tame a slope.

Retaining walls are bold architectural elements that create an intimate, enclosed atmosphere. Plants such as sedum, creeping phlox, or rock cress tumbling over the top of a wall soften the hard architectural lines and add color.

If one big wall won't do, several low walls with level terraces between may be the right solution. Consider paving a level to create a patio and a comfy seating area. An inviting midslope patio is an ideal place to sit and survey the rest of your garden.

Or you can plant a slope with groundcovers. Plant roots are very efficient at anchoring loose soil on a slope. Turn a tough hill into a beautiful planting by selecting easy-care groundcovers that root into the bank wherever their stems touch soil. The dense mats they create will reduce erosion and weeds.

Or you could go with a bolder approach, as in using boulders. Nestle clusters of boulders into the soil to anchor portions of the slope and add natural beauty. Arrange rocks into groups staggered informally for a natural look. Bury the bottom one-third to one-half of each large rock to stabilize it. Pack soil firmly around the rocks, and finish with plantings.

You could also consider a water feature. A shallow slope is the perfect site for a burbling stream and several small waterfalls. Cascading water spilling over slopes that once seemed unmanageable will also attract wildlife.

Use gravity to create a landscape asset by installing a waterfall, the ultimate way to take advantage of a slope. A steep slope is an opportunity to create a dramatic, sheer curtain of water. You'll need electricity nearby to bring life to the water pump, but a good electrician should be able to provide the power.

Beyond tilting the landscape, slopes create water-flow issues. Baffles, or miniature terraces, created with landscape edging or timbers set horizontally across a slope slow water runoff. While mulch tends to wash downhill on a bare slope, it stays in place when baffles help control the flow of water. Check for gullies after a heavy rainfall, and install additional baffles if needed.

opposite The back terrace replaced a dilapidated lawn and blackberry-blanketed slope with level, livable spaces. Large container plantings, including towering red bananas (*Ensete ventricosum* 'Maurelii'), bring season-long color to the space. **right** Favored for intimate dinners, this terrace features a see-through boundary of potted Madagascar dragontree (*Dracaena marginata*) that allows a tremendous view of Portland.

left Brick and stucco retaining walls extend elements of the home's architecture beyond the front courtyard and into the landscape. The garden's appeal lasts well into autumn thanks to long-blooming perennials, including golden black-eyed Susan (*Rudbeckia fulgida sullivantii* 'Goldsturm') and Frikart's aster (*Aster* × *frikartii* 'Mönch').

above Containers accent the steps that descend to the front courtyard from the driveway. The display of potted chrysanthemum, gloriosa daisy (*Rudbeckia hirta*), and leadwort (*Ceratostigma plumbaginoides*) adds lushness and color to the entryway.

USDA Plant Hardiness Zone Map

Each plant has an ability to withstand low temperatures. This range of temperatures is expressed as a Zone—and a Zone map shows where you can grow a plant.

Planting for your Zone

The U.S. Department of Agriculture designates 11 Zones from Canada to Mexico, and each represents the lowest expected winter temperature in that area. Each Zone is based on a 10°F difference in minimum temperatures. Once you know your hardiness Zone, you can choose plants for your garden that will flourish. Look for the hardiness Zone on the plant tags of the perennials, trees, and shrubs you buy.

Microclimates in your yard

Not all areas in your yard are the same. Depending on geography, trees, and structures, some spots may receive different sunlight and wind, and consequently experience temperature differences. Take a look around your yard, and you may notice that the same plant comes up sooner in one place than another. This is the microclimate concept in action. A microclimate is an area in your yard that is slightly different (cooler or warmer) than the other areas of your yard.

Create a microclimate

Once you're aware of your yard's microclimates, use them to your advantage. For example, you may be able to grow plants in a sheltered, south-facing garden bed that you can't grow elsewhere in your yard. You can create a microclimate by planting evergreens on the north side of a property to block prevailing winds. Or plant deciduous trees on the south side to provide shade in summer.

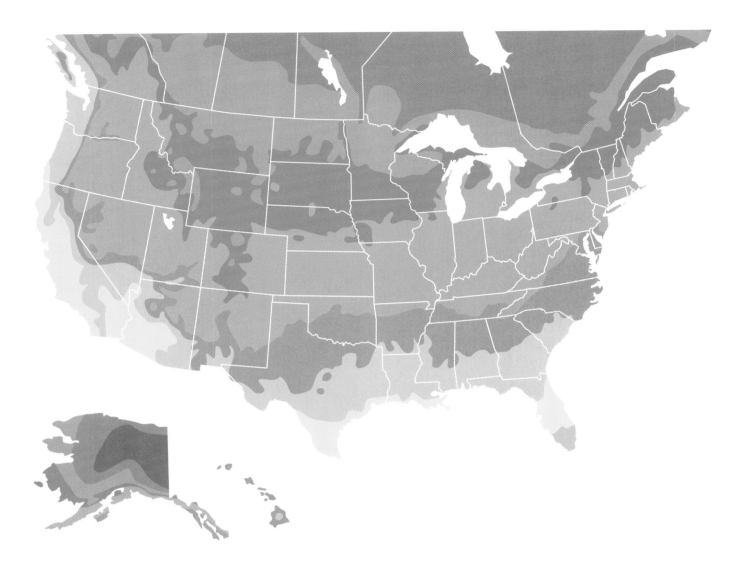

Range of Average Annual Minimum Temperatures for Each Zone

- Zone 1: below -50°F (below -45.6°C)
- Zone 2: -50 to -40°F (-45 to -40°C)
- Zone 3: -40 to -30°F (-40 to -35°C)
- Zone 4: -30 to -20°F (-34 to -29°C)
- Zone 5: -20 to -10°F (-29 to -23°C)
- Zone 6: -10 to 0°F (-23 to -18°C)
- Zone 7: 0 to 10°F (-18 to -12°C)
- Zone 8: 10 to 20°F (-12 to -7°C)
- Zone 9: 20 to 30°F (-7 to -1°C)
- Zone 10: 30 to 40°F (-1 to 4°C)
- Zone 11: 40°F and above (4.5°C and above)

opposite Spring gardens are awash in blue blooms. Iris, chives, and catmint are all early-spring perennial flowers.

Index

Page references in italics denote photographs.